SOFTWARE ENGINEERING
AND
TECH CULTURE
IN
NIGERIA

PEACE ISHOLA

Copyright © 2023 All rights reserved. Peace Ishola

No part of this book may be reproduced or transmitted in any form or by any means, electronic or mechanical, including photocopying, recording, or by any information storage and retrieval system, without permission in writing from the Copyright owner.

Any information is to be used for educational and information purposes only. It should never be substituted for financial advice.

The author or publisher does not in any way endorse any commercial products or services linked from other websites to this book.

Cover designed by:
Emphaloz Publishing House
www.emphaloz.com

ISBN: 978-2-7399-1467-4

A catalogue record of this book will be available from the National Library of Nigeria.

PREFACE

The Nigerian technology industry is one of the most dynamic and rapidly evolving sectors in the country. Over the past decade, it has transformed from a nascent industry into a significant driver of economic growth and innovation. This book, "Software Engineering and Tech Culture in Nigeria," aims to provide a comprehensive overview of the tech landscape in Nigeria, exploring its history, current state, and future prospects.

As an industry that is deeply intertwined with the cultural and socio-economic fabric of Nigeria, technology has the potential to address some of the country's most pressing challenges. From improving access to education and healthcare to driving financial inclusion and economic diversification, the tech industry is playing a pivotal role in shaping Nigeria's future.

The chapters in this book cover a wide range of topics, including the historical context of technology in Nigeria, the rise of tech hubs and innovation centers, the development of tech talent, the contributions of women in tech, the impact of fintech, healthtech, edtech, and agritech innovations, and the importance of cybersecurity and digital inclusion. Each chapter provides insights into the unique opportunities and challenges faced by Nigeria's tech industry and highlights the key players driving innovation and growth.

As you read through the chapters, you will gain a deeper understanding of how technology is transforming Nigeria and the factors that have contributed to its growth. You will also learn about the critical role of government policies, private sector initiatives, and international partnerships in fostering a vibrant and sustainable tech ecosystem.

This book is intended for anyone interested in understanding the Nigerian tech industry, including entrepreneurs, investors, policymakers, researchers, and students. It provides a comprehensive and in-depth analysis of the industry, offering valuable insights and practical knowledge that can inform decision-making and inspire further exploration.

I hope that this book will serve as a valuable resource for those seeking to understand and engage with Nigeria's tech industry. By highlighting the achievements, challenges, and opportunities in the sector, I aim to contribute to the ongoing dialogue about the role of technology in driving economic development and improving the quality of life in Nigeria.

Throughout the book, you will find detailed analysis, case studies, and insights from industry experts, providing a comprehensive and nuanced understanding of Nigeria's tech industry. Whether you are an entrepreneur, investor, policymaker, researcher, or student, this book offers valuable knowledge and practical insights that can inform your engagement with the Nigerian tech sector.

As Nigeria continues to navigate the complexities of modern technology and traditional culture, it stands as a testament to the power of cultural influence in shaping technological innovation. The preservation and integration of cultural values will ensure that technology remains relevant and beneficial to the people it serves.

In conclusion, the Nigerian tech industry is a dynamic and rapidly evolving sector with immense potential to drive economic growth and improve the quality of life for all Nigerians. By understanding its historical context, current state, and future prospects, we can appreciate the unique opportunities and challenges faced by the industry and contribute to its continued success and development.

Thank you for embarking on this journey to explore the fascinating world of technology and innovation in Nigeria. I hope that this book will inspire you to engage with the Nigerian tech industry, support its growth, and contribute to the vibrant and dynamic tech ecosystem that is shaping the future of Nigeria.

INTRODUCTION

Nigeria, often referred to as the "Giant of Africa," is a nation known for its rich cultural heritage, diverse population, and significant economic potential. Over the past decade, Nigeria has also emerged as a leading player in the African technology landscape. The tech industry in Nigeria has experienced remarkable growth, driven by a combination of entrepreneurial spirit, innovative solutions, and increasing access to digital technologies.

The purpose of this book is to provide a comprehensive overview of the Nigerian tech industry, exploring its historical development, current state, and future prospects. Through detailed analysis and insights, this book aims to highlight the unique opportunities and challenges faced by the industry and the key factors driving its growth.

The book begins with an exploration of the historical context of technology in Nigeria, tracing the evolution of indigenous knowledge and technological practices from pre-colonial times to the present day. Understanding this historical background is essential for appreciating the foundations upon which the modern tech industry has been built.

The subsequent chapters delve into various aspects of the tech industry, including the rise of tech hubs and innovation centers, the development of tech talent, and the contributions of women in tech. These chapters provide a detailed examination of the ecosystem that supports innovation and entrepreneurship in Nigeria, highlighting the key players and initiatives that have contributed to the industry's success.

The book also explores the impact of fintech, healthtech, edtech, and agritech innovations, showcasing how technology is transforming traditional sectors and addressing critical challenges in Nigeria. These chapters provide insights into the innovative solutions being developed and their potential to drive economic growth and improve the quality of life for Nigerians.

Cybersecurity and digital inclusion are also critical topics addressed in this book. As the tech industry grows, so do the challenges related to digital security and access. The chapters on cybersecurity and digital inclusion explore the risks and threats facing Nigeria, as well as the initiatives and measures being taken to protect data, ensure digital security, and promote equitable access to digital technologies.

The final chapters of the book look to the future, examining the opportunities and challenges that lie ahead for Nigeria's tech industry. By identifying key trends and emerging technologies, these chapters provide a roadmap for the continued growth and development of the sector.

Throughout the book, you will find detailed analysis, case studies, and insights from industry experts, providing a comprehensive and nuanced understanding of Nigeria's tech industry. Whether you are an entrepreneur, investor, policymaker, researcher, or student, this book offers valuable knowledge and practical insights that can inform your engagement with the Nigerian tech sector.

In conclusion, the Nigerian tech industry is a dynamic and rapidly evolving sector with immense potential to drive economic growth and improve the quality of life for all Nigerians. By understanding its historical context, current state, and future prospects, we can appreciate the unique opportunities and challenges faced by the industry and contribute to its continued success and development.

Thank you for embarking on this journey to explore the fascinating world of technology and innovation in Nigeria. I hope that this book will inspire you to engage with the Nigerian tech industry, support its growth, and contribute to the vibrant and dynamic tech ecosystem that is shaping the future of Nigeria.

By providing a comprehensive and in-depth analysis of the industry, this book aims to offer valuable insights and practical knowledge that can inform decision-making and inspire further exploration. Whether you are an entrepreneur looking to start a tech venture, an investor seeking opportunities in the Nigerian tech market, a policymaker aiming to create supportive policies for the tech sector, or a student interested in the future of technology in Nigeria, this book will serve as a valuable resource.

The Nigerian tech industry stands at a pivotal moment in its development, with the potential to become a global leader in innovation and technology. By leveraging its unique cultural heritage, fostering a supportive ecosystem, and addressing the challenges that lie ahead, Nigeria can achieve significant advancements in technology and contribute to the global digital economy.

As we explore the various aspects of the tech industry in Nigeria, we will see how technology is transforming lives, creating new opportunities, and driving economic growth. The stories of entrepreneurs, innovators, and leaders in the tech industry will inspire and motivate us to support the continued growth and success of Nigeria's tech ecosystem.

In conclusion, the Nigerian tech industry is a dynamic and rapidly evolving sector with immense potential to drive economic growth and improve the quality of life for all Nigerians. By understanding its historical context, current state, and future prospects, we can appreciate the unique opportunities and challenges faced by the industry and contribute to its continued success and development. Thank you for embarking on this journey to explore the fascinating world of technology and innovation in Nigeria.

I hope that this book will inspire you to engage with the Nigerian tech industry, support its growth, and contribute to the vibrant and dynamic tech ecosystem that is shaping the future of Nigeria.

With a deep understanding of the factors driving the growth of the Nigerian tech industry, we can work together to create a more inclusive, innovative, and prosperous future for all Nigerians. The journey of Nigeria's tech industry is just beginning, and the potential for growth and innovation is boundless. Let's embrace this exciting future and be part of the transformation that will define the next chapter of Nigeria's technological evolution.

CONTENTS

PREFACE iii
INTRODUCTION vii
CONTENTS xiii

CHAPTER 1
The Intersection of Culture and Technology in Nigeria 1

CHAPTER 2
Historical Context of Technology in Nigeria 10

CHAPTER 3
The Rise of Tech Hubs and Innovation Centers 21

CHAPTER 4
Education and Talent Development 31

CHAPTER 5
Women in Tech: Breaking Barriers and Shaping the Future 38

CHAPTER 6
Fintech Revolution: Transforming Financial Services 46

CHAPTER 7
Healthtech Innovations: Transforming Healthcare 56

CHAPTER 8
Edtech Innovations: Revolutionizing Education 66

CHAPTER 9
Agritech Innovations: Revolutionizing Agriculture 78

CHAPTER 10
Challenges Facing the Nigerian Tech Industry 88

CHAPTER 11
Government Policies Affecting the Tech Industry 96

CHAPTER 12
The Impact of the Tech Industry on Nigeria's Economy 105

CHAPTER 13
Digital Inclusion and Bridging the Digital Divide 111

CHAPTER 14
Cybersecurity and Data Privacy: Challenges and Solutions 118

CHAPTER 15
The Future of Nigeria's Tech Industry: Opportunities and
Challenges 125

CHAPTER 1

THE INTERSECTION OF CULTURE AND TECHNOLOGY IN NIGERIA

Nigeria, often referred to as the "Giant of Africa," is a nation rich in cultural heritage and diversity. With over 250 ethnic groups and a multitude of languages, Nigeria's culture plays a significant role in shaping its technological landscape. The intersection of culture and technology in Nigeria is a fascinating study of how traditional values and modern innovations coexist and influence each other. Cultural influences on technology adoption are evident in many facets of Nigerian society. The communal nature of Nigerian communities means that decisions are often made collectively, emphasizing the welfare of the community over individual interests. This communal approach extends to technology, where tech solutions that benefit the community as a whole are more likely to be accepted and adopted. For example, mobile payment solutions like Paga and Paystack have gained widespread acceptance because they facilitate easy and secure financial transactions within communities. These platforms are not just seen as tools for individual use but as enablers of community commerce and support systems.

Family and community ties are deeply ingrained in Nigerian culture, influencing the development of tech solutions that foster communication and connectivity. Social media platforms like WhatsApp and Facebook are immensely popular in Nigeria because they allow people to stay connected with family and friends, regardless of physical distance. These platforms have become virtual extensions of traditional community gatherings, where people can share news, celebrate milestones, and offer support. Traditional practices and modern innovations often coexist in Nigeria, creating unique opportunities for tech integration. For instance, traditional agriculture practices are being enhanced by modern agritech solutions. Farmers use mobile apps to access weather forecasts, market prices, and farming techniques, blending age-old knowledge with cutting-edge technology. Another example is the use of telemedicine to provide healthcare in remote areas. Traditional healers and community health workers are being trained to use mobile health platforms to diagnose and treat patients, ensuring that modern healthcare reaches even the most isolated communities.

Nollywood, Nigeria's vibrant film industry, is a prime example of how culture influences technology. Nollywood has not only become a cultural export but also a significant driver of tech adoption in Nigeria. The industry's demand for high-quality video production and distribution has spurred the development of tech solutions tailored to the entertainment sector. Streaming platforms like IrokoTV and YouTube have become popular channels for distributing Nollywood films, making them accessible to a global audience. The success of these platforms has also inspired tech entrepreneurs to develop local streaming services and content delivery networks, further integrating technology into Nigeria's cultural fabric. Language plays a crucial role in the adoption of technology in Nigeria. With so many languages spoken across the country, localization is vital for ensuring that tech solutions are accessible to a broad audience. Companies that invest in translating their platforms into local languages and adapting their content to cultural contexts are more likely to succeed. Google, for instance, has made significant efforts to localize its products for the Nigerian market. The company has introduced voice search in Nigerian Pidgin and translated its interfaces into major local languages such as Yoruba, Igbo, and Hausa. These efforts have increased the accessibility and usability of Google's products, making them more relevant to Nigerian users.

Cultural challenges often drive innovation in Nigeria. The need to address specific cultural and societal issues has led to the development of unique tech solutions. For example, the high cost of textbooks and educational materials in Nigeria has driven the growth of edtech platforms like Tuteria and uLesson, which provide affordable and accessible educational content. Similarly, the importance of community support in Nigerian culture has inspired the creation of crowdfunding platforms tailored to local needs. Platforms like NaijaFund and DonateNG enable Nigerians to raise funds for community projects, medical expenses, and educational pursuits, leveraging the communal spirit to solve financial challenges. The future of culture and technology in Nigeria is bright, with both elements continuing to influence and shape each other. As technology becomes more ingrained in everyday life, it will be crucial to preserve and integrate cultural values to ensure that tech solutions remain relevant and beneficial. One promising area is the development of culturally relevant AI and machine learning applications. By training AI models on local languages and cultural nuances, Nigerian tech companies can create more intuitive and effective solutions for various sectors, from healthcare to education. Additionally, the growing focus on digital inclusion and literacy will ensure that more Nigerians, regardless of their cultural background or location, can participate in the tech revolution. Initiatives like the National Digital Economy Policy and Strategy aim to bridge the digital divide and empower all Nigerians to leverage technology for personal and community development.

The intersection of culture and technology in Nigeria is a dynamic and evolving landscape. Cultural values, social norms, and traditional practices continue to influence the development and adoption of technology, creating a unique and vibrant tech ecosystem. By embracing and integrating these cultural elements, Nigeria's tech industry can foster innovation that is not only cutting-edge but also deeply rooted in the fabric of Nigerian society. The preservation and integration of cultural values will ensure that technology remains relevant and beneficial to the people it serves. As Nigeria continues to navigate the complexities of modern technology and traditional culture, the nation stands as a testament to the power of cultural influence in shaping technological innovation.

The influence of religion on technology in Nigeria is another critical aspect to consider. Nigeria is a deeply religious country with Christianity and Islam being the predominant religions. Religious beliefs and practices often intersect with technological adoption and usage. For instance, many churches and mosques in Nigeria have embraced digital technologies to reach their congregations. Live streaming of religious services, online donations, and mobile apps for religious education are becoming increasingly common. These technological integrations have allowed religious institutions to maintain their influence and relevance in a rapidly changing digital world.

Moreover, religious organizations are also playing a role in promoting digital literacy and technology adoption. Various religious groups have initiated programs to teach digital skills to their members, recognizing the importance of technology in today's society. This blend of faith and technology ensures that even deeply traditional aspects of Nigerian culture are not left behind in the digital revolution.

In the realm of fashion, Nigerian culture is making its mark on technology through the fusion of traditional designs with modern e-commerce platforms. The Nigerian fashion industry, known for its vibrant and diverse styles, has embraced technology to reach global markets. Online fashion stores and social media platforms are being used to showcase Nigerian designs, making it easier for local designers to gain international recognition. This digital transformation in the fashion industry not only preserves traditional Nigerian designs but also propels them onto the global stage, demonstrating how technology can amplify cultural heritage.

Furthermore, the Nigerian diaspora plays a significant role in the intersection of culture and technology. Nigerians living abroad are leveraging technology to stay connected with their homeland and contribute to its development. Remittance platforms, diaspora investment initiatives, and online cultural communities are some of the ways the diaspora is using technology to maintain cultural ties and support economic growth in Nigeria. These digital connections ensure that the cultural influence of the Nigerian diaspora continues to shape and enhance the technological landscape back home.

Finally, the integration of traditional crafts and modern technology is another exciting development in Nigeria. Artisans and craftsmen are using digital platforms to market and sell their products, reaching customers beyond their local communities. Online marketplaces and social media have provided a global stage for Nigerian crafts, preserving traditional skills while adapting to the demands of the modern market. This intersection of culture and technology ensures that traditional crafts remain relevant and economically viable in the digital age.

In conclusion, the intersection of culture and technology in Nigeria is multifaceted and dynamic. Cultural values, social norms, traditional practices, religion, fashion, and the diaspora all play crucial roles in shaping the technological landscape. By embracing these cultural elements and integrating them with modern technology, Nigeria is creating a unique and vibrant tech ecosystem that is deeply rooted in its rich heritage. The continued preservation and integration of cultural values will ensure that technological innovations remain relevant and beneficial to all Nigerians, driving sustainable growth and development.

CHAPTER 2

HISTORICAL CONTEXT OF TECHNOLOGY IN NIGERIA

To understand the current state of technology in Nigeria, it is essential to delve into its historical context. The evolution of technology in Nigeria has been shaped by a series of significant events and influences, from pre-colonial times to the present day. This chapter explores the historical milestones that have paved the way for Nigeria's technological advancements. Long before the advent of modern technology, Nigeria had a rich tradition of indigenous knowledge and technological practices. Various ethnic groups developed sophisticated agricultural techniques, metalworking skills, and architectural innovations. These indigenous technologies were well-suited to the local environment and played a crucial role in sustaining communities. For example, the Yoruba people developed advanced iron smelting techniques, producing high-quality iron tools and weapons. The Benin Empire was renowned for its bronze casting and intricate sculptures, which remain highly regarded in the art world today. These early technological achievements laid the foundation for future innovations.

The arrival of European colonizers in the late 19th century brought significant changes to Nigeria's technological landscape. The colonial era introduced new technologies and infrastructures, such as railways, telecommunication systems, and mechanized agriculture. While these developments had a profound impact, they also disrupted traditional practices and knowledge systems. Colonial policies often prioritized the extraction of resources and the establishment of infrastructure to serve colonial interests. This focus on resource exploitation and export-oriented agriculture led to the marginalization of indigenous technologies and the imposition of foreign technological paradigms. Nigeria's independence in 1960 marked a new chapter in its technological journey. The post-independence era saw efforts to reclaim and adapt traditional knowledge while embracing modern technologies. The government invested in infrastructure development, education, and industrialization to drive technological progress. The establishment of universities and research institutions played a crucial role in advancing technology. Institutions like the University of Lagos, Ahmadu Bello University, and the Obafemi Awolowo University became centers of excellence in science and technology education. These institutions produced a new generation of scientists, engineers, and technologists who contributed to Nigeria's technological growth.

The discovery of oil in commercial quantities in the late 1950s and the subsequent oil boom of the 1970s brought unprecedented wealth to Nigeria. This newfound wealth provided the government with the resources to invest in technological infrastructure and industrial development. During this period, Nigeria made significant investments in the energy sector, building refineries, power plants, and pipelines. The oil revenue also funded the construction of roads, bridges, and telecommunications infrastructure, laying the groundwork for modern technological advancements. The late 20th and early 21st centuries witnessed the rapid rise of information and communication technology (ICT) in Nigeria. The liberalization of the telecommunications sector in the early 2000s was a turning point, leading to the proliferation of mobile phones and internet access. The advent of mobile technology revolutionized communication in Nigeria, making it more accessible and affordable. The widespread adoption of mobile phones created new opportunities for tech entrepreneurs to develop mobile-based solutions for various sectors, including finance, healthcare, and agriculture.

The early 2010s marked the birth of Nigeria's vibrant tech ecosystem. The establishment of tech hubs and innovation centers, such as Co-Creation Hub (CcHub) in Lagos, provided a supportive environment for startups and tech enthusiasts. These hubs offered resources, mentorship, and networking opportunities, fostering innovation and entrepreneurship. The success of early tech startups like Jobberman, an online job portal, and IrokoTV, a streaming service for Nollywood films, demonstrated the potential of Nigeria's tech industry. These startups attracted significant investments and inspired a new wave of tech entrepreneurs to pursue their innovative ideas. Government policies and initiatives have played a crucial role in shaping Nigeria's tech landscape. The National Information Technology Development Agency (NITDA) was established in 2001 to oversee the development of IT in the country. NITDA's policies and programs, such as the National Broadband Plan and the Nigeria ICT Innovation and Entrepreneurship Vision (NIIEV), have provided a framework for tech growth. Additionally, the government's focus on digital inclusion and literacy has aimed to bridge the digital divide and empower all Nigerians to participate in the tech economy. Programs like the Digital Nigeria Project and various e-government initiatives have sought to enhance digital skills and promote the adoption of technology in public services.

Despite the progress made, Nigeria's tech industry faces several challenges that must be addressed to ensure sustained growth and development. One of the primary challenges is the need for continuous investment in digital infrastructure. Improving internet connectivity, power supply, and technology access is crucial for the development of the tech industry. Addressing the talent gap remains a priority. Efforts to enhance tech education, provide training opportunities, and retain top talent are essential. Collaborative initiatives between the government, private sector, and educational institutions can help bridge the talent gap and ensure a steady supply of skilled software engineers. Regulatory challenges also need to be addressed to create a more conducive environment for tech innovation. Streamlining regulations, reducing bureaucratic hurdles, and providing clear guidelines for tech companies can foster a more business-friendly environment. Cybersecurity is another significant challenge. As the tech industry grows, so does the risk of cyber threats. Ensuring robust cyber security measures and educating users about digital security will be critical in protecting data and maintaining trust in digital solutions.

The story of technology in Nigeria is one of resilience, adaptation, and innovation. From the sophisticated agricultural techniques of pre-colonial times to the cutting-edge innovations of today, Nigeria's technological journey has been shaped by its unique cultural and historical context. The future of technology in Nigeria looks promising, with continued investments in infrastructure, education, and innovation. As the country navigates the challenges and opportunities of the digital age, it stands poised to make significant contributions to the global tech landscape. By leveraging its rich cultural heritage and embracing modern technological advancements, Nigeria can build a sustainable and inclusive tech ecosystem that benefits all its citizens.

The role of education in shaping Nigeria's technological landscape cannot be overstated. Over the years, Nigerian educational institutions have produced a significant number of scientists, engineers, and technologists who have gone on to make substantial contributions to various fields. The government's investment in science and technology education has been pivotal in building a knowledgeable workforce capable of driving technological innovation. Furthermore, the establishment of specialized institutions like the Nigerian Institute of Science Laboratory Technology (NISLT) and the National Mathematical Centre (NMC) has further strengthened Nigeria's capacity to innovate and develop new technologies. These institutions have provided a platform for research and development, fostering a culture of scientific inquiry and technological advancement.

The impact of international collaborations on Nigeria's technological development is also noteworthy. Over the years, Nigeria has partnered with various countries and international organizations to enhance its technological capabilities. For instance, collaborations with countries like China, India, and the United States have facilitated the transfer of technology and knowledge, contributing to the growth of Nigeria's tech industry. International organizations like the United Nations Development Programme (UNDP) and the World Bank have also played a crucial role in supporting Nigeria's technological development. These organizations have provided funding, technical assistance, and capacity-building programs to help Nigeria address its technological challenges and leverage new opportunities.

The role of the private sector in driving technological innovation in Nigeria is significant. Private companies, both local and international, have made substantial investments in Nigeria's tech industry, contributing to its growth and development. Companies like MTN, Airtel, and Globacom have played a crucial role in expanding internet connectivity and mobile phone penetration, laying the foundation for the growth of the tech ecosystem. Furthermore, tech giants like Google, Microsoft, and Facebook have made significant investments in Nigeria, supporting local startups and promoting digital literacy and skills development. These companies have established partnerships with local organizations, providing funding, resources, and mentorship to help Nigerian tech entrepreneurs succeed.

The rise of tech entrepreneurship in Nigeria is a testament to the country's innovative spirit. Nigerian tech entrepreneurs have developed groundbreaking solutions to address local challenges, from mobile banking and e-commerce to healthtech and agritech. These entrepreneurs have demonstrated resilience and creativity, navigating a complex and often challenging business environment to build successful tech companies. Tech hubs and innovation centers have played a crucial role in supporting these entrepreneurs, providing a collaborative environment where ideas can flourish and grow. These hubs offer resources, mentorship, and networking opportunities, helping startups overcome challenges and scale their operations.

The impact of technology on various sectors in Nigeria is profound. In agriculture, technology has revolutionized farming practices, improving productivity and sustainability. Agritech solutions like Farmcrowdy and ThriveAgric have provided farmers with access to funding, market information, and modern farming techniques, transforming the agricultural sector. In healthcare, technology has improved access to medical services and enhanced the quality of care. Healthtech companies like LifeBank and 54gene have leveraged technology to address critical healthcare challenges, from delivering medical supplies to advancing genomics research.

In education, technology has made learning more accessible and engaging. Edtech platforms like uLesson and Tuteria have provided students with innovative learning solutions, improving educational outcomes and addressing the challenges of traditional education. In finance, fintech companies have revolutionized financial services, making banking more accessible and efficient. Companies like Paystack and Flutterwave have developed innovative payment solutions, promoted financial inclusion and drove economic growth.

In conclusion, the historical context of technology in Nigeria provides valuable insights into the factors that have shaped its technological landscape. From indigenous knowledge and colonial influences to post-independence developments and the rise of the digital age, Nigeria's technological journey is a story of resilience, adaptation, and innovation. By understanding this historical context, we can appreciate the unique opportunities and challenges faced by Nigeria's tech industry and contribute to its continued growth and development. The future of technology in Nigeria is bright, with continued investments in infrastructure, education, and innovation expected to drive further advancements and create a more inclusive and prosperous society.

CHAPTER 3

THE RISE OF TECH HUBS AND INNOVATION CENTERS

The emergence of tech hubs and innovation centers has been pivotal in Nigeria's tech boom. These centers provide a supportive environment for startups, offering resources, mentorship, and networking opportunities. The rise of tech hubs like Co-Creation Hub (CcHub) in Lagos has transformed the landscape of Nigerian technology, fostering innovation and entrepreneurship. Tech hubs have become the epicenters of technological innovation in Nigeria. They provide a collaborative space where tech enthusiasts, entrepreneurs, and investors can connect and innovate.

These hubs offer a range of services, including incubation programs, funding support, and access to cutting-edge technology. By bringing together diverse talents and resources, tech hubs create an environment conducive to creativity and problem-solving.

Co-Creation Hub (CcHub) is one of the most prominent tech hubs in Nigeria. Established in 2010, CcHub has played a crucial role in nurturing startups and fostering a culture of innovation. Located in Yaba, Lagos, CcHub provides a collaborative workspace, access to funding, and mentorship from experienced professionals. The hub has supported numerous successful startups, including BudgIT, a civic tech organization that uses technology to simplify government budgets and public finance data. Another notable tech hub is the Wennovation Hub, which focuses on driving social impact through innovation and entrepreneurship. The hub provides training, mentorship, and funding to startups working on solutions in health, education, and agriculture. Wennovation Hub's emphasis on social impact aligns with the communal values of Nigerian culture, fostering innovations that benefit society as a whole.

Tech hubs also play a vital role in bridging the gap between academia and industry. They collaborate with universities and research institutions to provide students with practical experience and exposure to real-world challenges. These partnerships facilitate the transfer of knowledge and technology, enhancing the quality of tech education and training. For example, the Lagos Innovation Council, a government initiative, collaborates with tech hubs and universities to promote research and development in technology. The council provides funding for innovative projects and facilitates partnerships between academia and industry. These initiatives ensure that students are well-prepared to enter the tech workforce and contribute to the growth of the industry.

The success of tech hubs in Nigeria has attracted significant investments from both local and international sources. Venture capital firms, angel investors, and development organizations recognize the potential of Nigerian tech startups and are eager to support their growth. This influx of funding has enabled startups to scale their operations, develop new products, and expand their market reach. International partnerships have also played a crucial role in the growth of tech hubs. For instance,

CcHub has partnered with organizations like Google for Startups and Facebook to provide additional resources and support to Nigerian startups. These partnerships offer access to global networks, mentorship from industry experts, and opportunities for international exposure.

Tech hubs have also contributed to the rise of female entrepreneurs in Nigeria. Initiatives like She Leads Africa and Women in Tech Africa provide support and resources to women in the tech industry. These organizations offer mentorship, training, and networking opportunities, empowering women to pursue careers in technology and entrepreneurship. She Leads Africa, for example, runs a digital accelerator program that supports female-led startups with training, mentorship, and access to funding. The program has helped numerous women launch successful tech ventures and make significant contributions to the industry. Women in Tech Africa, a pan-African organization, focuses on promoting gender diversity and inclusion in the tech sector. The organization hosts events, workshops, and mentorship programs to support women in technology and create a more inclusive tech ecosystem.

The impact of tech hubs extends beyond the tech industry, influencing other sectors such as agriculture, healthcare, and education. Agritech startups like Farmcrowdy and ThriveAgric are using technology to transform agriculture in Nigeria. These startups provide farmers with access to funding, market information, and modern farming techniques, improving productivity and sustainability. Healthtech startups like LifeBank and 54gene are leveraging technology to address healthcare challenges in Nigeria. LifeBank uses technology to deliver essential medical supplies, including blood and oxygen, to hospitals. The company's innovative approach has saved countless lives and earned international recognition. 54gene, a genomics research company, is advancing medical research in Africa by collecting and analyzing genetic data from diverse populations. The company's work has the potential to improve healthcare outcomes and contribute to global medical research.

Edtech startups like uLesson and Tuteria are using technology to enhance education in Nigeria. uLesson provides video lessons and interactive quizzes for primary and secondary school students, making education more accessible and engaging. Tuteria connects students with qualified tutors for one-on-one lessons, improving the quality of education and helping students achieve their academic goals. The future of tech hubs and innovation centers in Nigeria looks promising. As the tech ecosystem continues to grow, these hubs will play an increasingly important role in nurturing talent, fostering innovation, and driving economic development. By providing a supportive environment for startups and promoting collaboration between academia, industry, and government, tech hubs are laying the foundation for a vibrant and sustainable tech ecosystem.

In conclusion, the rise of tech hubs and innovation centers has been a game-changer for Nigeria's tech industry. These hubs provide the resources, mentorship, and collaborative environment needed to foster innovation and entrepreneurship. They have nurtured successful startups, attracted significant investments, and bridged the gap between academia and industry. As Nigeria continues to navigate the challenges and opportunities of the digital age, tech hubs will remain at the forefront of technological innovation and economic development. The story of tech hubs in Nigeria is a testament to the power of collaboration and community in driving technological progress. By fostering an environment where ideas can flourish and entrepreneurs can thrive, these hubs are helping to shape the future of technology in Nigeria.

The role of government support in the growth of tech hubs cannot be overlooked. Various government initiatives have been instrumental in creating an enabling environment for tech hubs to thrive. For instance, the National Information Technology Development Agency (NITDA) has launched programs to support tech startups and innovation hubs, providing funding, resources, and policy support. The Lagos State government has also played a proactive role in supporting the tech ecosystem. Initiatives like the Lagos Innovates program provide co-working grants, accelerator grants, and workspace vouchers to support tech startups and innovation centers. These initiatives have helped to create a thriving tech community in Lagos, often referred to as the "Silicon Valley of Africa."

Furthermore, the role of international collaborations and partnerships in the growth of tech hubs is significant. Global tech giants like Google, Microsoft, and Facebook have established partnerships with Nigerian tech hubs to provide mentorship, funding, and resources. These partnerships have not only provided Nigerian startups with access to global expertise and networks but have also attracted international attention to Nigeria's burgeoning tech ecosystem. For example, Google's Launchpad Accelerator program has supported several Nigerian startups, providing them with mentorship, funding, and access to Google's resources. Similarly, Facebook's NG_Hub in Lagos serves as a center for collaboration, training, and networking, supporting the growth of the tech ecosystem.

The impact of tech hubs on job creation and economic development is profound. By supporting startups and fostering innovation, tech hubs have created numerous job opportunities for young Nigerians. These jobs range from software development and digital marketing to project management and customer support. The ripple effect of job creation extends to other sectors, such as finance, logistics, and retail, contributing to overall economic growth. Tech hubs have also played a crucial role in addressing social and developmental challenges in Nigeria. By supporting startups focused on sectors like healthcare, education, and agriculture, tech hubs are driving innovations that address critical societal issues. For instance, healthtech startups supported by tech hubs are developing solutions to improve access to healthcare, particularly in rural and underserved areas. Edtech startups are leveraging technology to enhance educational outcomes and bridge the gap in access to quality education.

The success stories of startups emerging from Nigerian tech hubs are inspiring. Companies like Flutterwave, Andela, and Paystack have not only achieved significant success but have also put Nigeria on the global tech map. These startups have attracted substantial investments, created thousands of jobs, and demonstrated the potential of Nigerian tech talent. Flutterwave, for example, has revolutionized online payments in Africa, providing a platform for businesses to accept payments from customers across the continent. Andela has trained and placed thousands of software developers with global tech companies, addressing the global tech talent shortage. Paystack, acquired by Stripe for $200 million, has developed innovative payment solutions that have transformed digital transactions in Nigeria.

In conclusion, the rise of tech hubs and innovation centers has been a catalyst for the growth of Nigeria's tech industry. These hubs provide a supportive environment for startups, foster innovation, and drive economic development. By bringing together diverse talents and resources, tech hubs create a collaborative space where ideas can flourish and entrepreneurs can succeed. The story of tech hubs in Nigeria is a testament to the power of community, collaboration, and innovation in driving technological progress. As Nigeria continues to navigate the digital age, tech hubs will remain at the forefront of technological innovation and economic development, shaping the future of technology in the country.

CHAPTER 4

EDUCATION AND TALENT DEVELOPMENT

Education is the cornerstone of any thriving tech ecosystem. In Nigeria, the state of tech education has undergone significant transformation over the years, from traditional universities to coding bootcamps and online learning platforms. The development of tech talent is crucial for the growth of the industry, and this chapter examines the challenges and opportunities in tech education, the role of government policies, and the impact of private sector initiatives. Traditional universities have been the primary sources of formal education in technology-related fields. Leading institutions like the

University of Lagos, Ahmadu Bello University, and the Federal University of Technology, Akure, offer programs in computer science, engineering, and information technology. These institutions provide a solid foundation in theoretical and practical aspects of technology, equipping students with the skills needed to thrive in the tech industry.

However, the formal education system faces several challenges, including outdated curricula, inadequate infrastructure, and limited industry collaboration. To address these issues, universities are increasingly partnering with tech companies and innovation hubs to enhance their programs. These partnerships provide students with practical experience, exposure to real-world challenges, and access to cutting-edge technology. Coding bootcamps and online learning platforms have emerged as important players in tech education. Organizations like Andela, Decagon, and Semicolon offer intensive training programs that focus on practical coding skills and real-world experience. These programs are designed to bridge the gap between formal education and industry requirements, providing students with the skills needed to excel in the tech industry.

Andela, for example, identifies talented individuals through a rigorous selection process and provides them with advanced training in software development. The program includes hands-on projects, mentorship, and placement with global tech companies. Andela's innovative model addresses the global talent shortage by tapping into the underutilized pool of African developers and connecting them with international opportunities. Decagon offers a six-month intensive software engineering program that combines classroom learning with practical experience. The program covers various programming languages and technologies, preparing participants for careers in software development. Decagon also provides job placement support to help graduates find employment in the tech industry.

Online learning platforms like Coursera, Udemy, and freeCodeCamp have democratized access to quality tech education, enabling individuals to learn at their own pace and convenience. These platforms offer courses on various programming languages, frameworks, and tools, providing a flexible and cost-effective way for aspiring software engineers to acquire new skills or enhance existing ones. Coursera partners with top universities and organizations to offer online courses, specializations, and degrees. The platform covers a wide range of tech topics, including programming, data science, and artificial intelligence. Coursera's courses are designed to be accessible and affordable, making quality education available to a global audience. Udemy is an online learning platform that offers courses on a variety of subjects, including software development, data science, and cybersecurity. The platform allows instructors to create and share their courses, providing a diverse range of learning opportunities. Udemy's courses are often project-based, enabling learners to apply their knowledge in practical scenarios.

FreeCodeCamp is a nonprofit organization that offers free coding education through an interactive online platform. The platform provides a comprehensive curriculum covering web development, data visualization, and machine learning. FreeCodeCamp also includes real-world projects and a supportive community, helping learners gain hands-on experience and build a portfolio. Mentorship plays a crucial role in the development of tech talent in Nigeria. Experienced professionals and industry leaders often take on mentorship roles, guiding and supporting aspiring engineers. Mentorship provides learners with insights into industry best practices, career advice, and technical guidance. It also helps mentees build professional networks, which can be instrumental in securing job opportunities and advancing their careers.

Professional development is also supported through conferences, hackathons, and tech meetups. Events such as the Lagos Startup Week, Google Developer Group (GDG) meetups, and Facebook Developer Circles provide platforms for knowledge sharing, networking, and collaboration. These events allow software engineers to stay updated on the latest industry trends, learn from peers, and showcase their skills. Despite the progress made in tech education, Nigeria still faces a significant talent gap in software engineering. This gap is characterized by a shortage of skilled professionals needed to meet the growing demands of the tech industry. Several factors contribute to this talent gap, including the rapid pace of technological advancements, limited access to quality education, and brain drain.

To address this gap, various initiatives have been implemented to enhance tech education and training. Government policies, private sector investments, and international collaborations are all contributing to the development of a robust talent pipeline. For example, the National Information Technology Development Agency (NITDA) offers scholarships and grants to support tech education and research. Private sector initiatives, such as the Google Africa Developer Scholarship and Facebook's Developer Circles, provide training and mentorship opportunities to aspiring software engineers. These programs aim to equip individuals with the skills needed to succeed in the tech industry and contribute to the overall growth of the ecosystem.

The future of tech education and talent development in Nigeria is promising. Continued investments in education, training, and mentorship will ensure a steady supply of skilled professionals to meet the demands of the growing tech industry. By fostering a culture of continuous learning and development, Nigeria can build a robust and dynamic tech ecosystem that drives innovation and economic growth. The country's tech industry has the potential to become a global powerhouse, with Nigerian software engineers and technologists leading the way in innovation and technological advancement.

In conclusion, the development of tech talent in Nigeria is critical for the growth and success of the tech industry. By addressing the challenges in tech education and investing in training, mentorship, and professional development, Nigeria can build a thriving tech ecosystem that drives innovation and economic development. The future of tech education in Nigeria is bright, with continued efforts to enhance the quality and accessibility of education, foster a culture of continuous learning, and support the growth of the tech industry.

CHAPTER 5

WOMEN IN TECH: BREAKING BARRIERS AND SHAPING THE FUTURE

Women in Nigeria's tech industry face unique challenges but also have incredible stories of success and resilience. This chapter focuses on the contributions of women in tech, profiling influential female tech leaders and entrepreneurs. We explore the barriers they face, the initiatives supporting gender diversity, and the inspiring journeys of women who are breaking stereotypes and leading the way in tech innovation. Women have made significant contributions to Nigeria's tech industry, breaking barriers and challenging stereotypes. Despite facing numerous challenges, Nigerian women in tech have demonstrated resilience, creativity, and leadership, paving the way for future generations. Their involvement spans various roles, including software development, data science, cybersecurity, and tech entrepreneurship.

Prominent women in tech, such as Ommo Clark, CEO of iBez, and Rebecca Enonchong, founder of AppsTech, serve as role models and inspire other women to pursue careers in technology. Their achievements highlight the potential and impact of women in the tech industry and underscore the importance of diversity and inclusion. Ommo Clark is the founder and CEO of iBez, a software development company that creates solutions for small and medium-sized enterprises (SMEs). With a background in software engineering and a passion for entrepreneurship, Ommo has led iBez to develop innovative products that address the needs of local businesses. Her work has earned her recognition as a leading female tech entrepreneur in Nigeria. Rebecca Enonchong, although based in Cameroon, has made a significant impact on the African tech scene, including Nigeria. As the founder of AppsTech, a global provider of enterprise software solutions, Rebecca has been a vocal advocate for women in tech and has supported numerous initiatives to promote diversity in the industry. Her leadership and advocacy have inspired many women across Africa to pursue careers in technology.

Ire Aderinokun is Nigeria's first female Google Developer Expert in web technologies. She is known for her contributions to the tech community through her blog, speaking engagements, and active participation in developer forums. Ire has been a strong advocate for women in tech and has inspired many young women to pursue careers in software development. Her work focuses on front-end development, and she has made significant contributions to improving web accessibility and performance. Temie Giwa-Tubosun is the founder of LifeBank, a healthtech company that uses technology to deliver essential medical supplies, including blood and oxygen, to hospitals in Nigeria. Temie's innovative approach to solving healthcare challenges has saved numerous lives and has earned her international recognition. She is a passionate advocate for women in tech and healthcare, emphasizing the importance of leveraging technology to address critical issues in society. Abisoye Ajayi-Akinfolarin is the founder of Pearls Africa

Youth Foundation, an organization that provides technology training and mentorship to young girls in underserved communities. Through her initiatives, Abisoye has empowered many girls with the skills and confidence needed to pursue careers in tech. She has received numerous awards for her work, including being named one of CNN's Heroes.

Despite their achievements, women in Nigeria's tech industry face several challenges, including gender bias, limited access to funding, and societal expectations. These challenges often result in underrepresentation and limited career advancement opportunities for women in tech. Various initiatives have been established to address these challenges and promote gender diversity in the tech industry. Organizations like She Leads Africa, Women in Tech Africa, and TechHer are dedicated to supporting and empowering women in tech. These organizations provide mentorship, training, networking opportunities, and advocacy to help women overcome barriers and succeed in their careers. She Leads Africa is an organization that supports young African women in entrepreneurship and professional development. Through its programs, She Leads Africa provides mentorship, training, and funding opportunities to women in tech. The organization aims to create a community of women who can support each other and drive change in the tech industry.

Women in Tech Africa is a pan-African organization that focuses on promoting women's participation in technology. The organization offers various programs, including mentorship, training workshops, and networking events. Women in Tech Africa also advocates for policies that support gender diversity and inclusion in the tech industry. TechHer is an organization that aims to close the gender gap in technology by providing women with the skills, knowledge, and support needed to thrive in the tech industry. TechHer offers coding bootcamps, mentorship programs, and community events to empower women and create a supportive network for their professional growth. Success stories of women in tech serve as powerful motivators and sources of inspiration for aspiring female engineers and entrepreneurs. For example, Ire Aderinokun, Nigeria's first female Google Developer Expert in web technologies, has made significant contributions to the tech community through her work and advocacy for women in tech.

Mentorship programs specifically designed for women are instrumental in fostering their growth and development. Programs like TechWomen and the African Women in Tech (AWIT) mentorship initiative connect aspiring female tech professionals with experienced mentors who provide guidance, support, and career advice. These mentorship relationships help women navigate the challenges of the tech industry and build successful careers. TechWomen is a U.S. Department of State initiative that connects women in STEM fields from Africa, Central Asia, and the Middle East with professional mentors in the United States. The program includes mentorship, networking, and cultural exchange, helping participants gain new skills and perspectives. TechWomen has supported many Nigerian women in tech, providing them with the tools and support needed to advance their careers.

AWIT is a mentorship program that connects aspiring female tech professionals with experienced mentors across Africa. The program provides one-on-one mentorship, group workshops, and networking opportunities. AWIT aims to empower women in tech by providing them with the guidance and support needed to overcome challenges and achieve their professional goals. The future of women in Nigerian software engineering is promising, with increasing efforts to promote gender diversity and inclusion. As more women enter the tech industry and achieve success, they pave the way for future generations. The growing awareness of the importance of diversity in driving innovation and business success is also contributing to a more inclusive tech ecosystem.

Continued investment in education, mentorship, and advocacy is essential to ensure that women have equal opportunities to thrive in the tech industry. By addressing gender biases, providing access to resources, and creating supportive networks, Nigeria can harness the full potential of its female tech talent and drive further innovation and growth in the sector. The success of women in Nigeria's tech industry demonstrates the transformative power of diversity and inclusion. By fostering a culture that values and supports women in tech, Nigeria can build a stronger, more innovative, and competitive tech ecosystem that benefits all its citizens.

In conclusion, women in Nigeria's tech industry are breaking barriers and shaping the future of technology. Despite facing numerous challenges, they have made significant contributions and achieved remarkable success. By supporting initiatives that promote gender diversity, providing mentorship and resources, and creating an inclusive environment, Nigeria can empower more women to pursue careers in tech and drive further innovation and growth in the sector. The future of women in tech in Nigeria is bright, with continued efforts to promote diversity and inclusion expected to yield even greater achievements and advancements.

CHAPTER 6

FINTECH REVOLUTION: TRANSFORMING FINANCIAL SERVICES

The fintech sector in Nigeria has experienced explosive growth, revolutionized financial services and promoted financial inclusion. This chapter delves into the rise of fintech companies such as Paystack, Flutterwave, and Paga. We explore how these companies are leveraging technology to provide innovative financial solutions, the challenges they face, and their impact on the economy and society. Fintech, short for financial technology, refers to the use of technology to improve and automate financial services. In Nigeria, the fintech revolution has been driven by the need to address the challenges of financial inclusion and provide convenient and accessible financial services to a large, underserved population.

Paystack, founded by Shola Akinlade and Ezra Olubi in 2015, has revolutionized online payments in Nigeria. The company's platform enables businesses to accept payments from customers via multiple channels, including cards, bank transfers, and mobile money. Paystack's user-friendly interface, reliable service, and robust security features have made it a popular choice for businesses of all sizes. In 2020, Paystack was acquired by Stripe, a global payments company, for $200 million, marking one of the largest exits in the African tech scene. Flutterwave, co-founded by Iyinoluwa Aboyeji and Olugbenga Agboola in 2016, is another leading fintech company in Nigeria. Flutterwave provides a payment infrastructure for global merchants and payment service providers. The company's platform facilitates seamless payments across different channels and currencies, making it easier for businesses to operate in multiple markets. Flutterwave's solutions have been integrated by major companies like Uber and Facebook, demonstrating the company's impact on the global payments landscape.

Paga, founded by Tayo Oviosu in 2009, aims to make financial services accessible to everyone. Paga's mobile wallet allows users to send and receive money, pay bills, and make purchases. The company has built an extensive agent network, enabling users to perform transactions at local shops and kiosks. Paga's focus on financial inclusion has helped millions of Nigerians access essential financial services, particularly in rural areas. The success of these fintech companies has had a significant impact on the Nigerian economy. By providing innovative financial solutions, fintech companies have enabled businesses to operate more efficiently, reduced transaction costs, and increased access to financial services. This has led to the growth of the digital economy and created new opportunities for entrepreneurship and job creation.

The rise of fintech has also promoted financial inclusion, a critical issue in Nigeria, where a large portion of the population remains unbanked or underbanked. Fintech solutions have made it easier for people to access banking services, save money, and obtain credit. This has empowered individuals and small businesses, contributing to economic development and poverty reduction. Despite their success, fintech companies in Nigeria face several challenges. Regulatory compliance is a significant concern, as the financial industry is heavily regulated. Fintech companies must navigate complex regulatory requirements to ensure their operations comply with the law. Additionally, the rapid pace of technological change requires continuous innovation and adaptation to stay competitive.

Infrastructure challenges, such as unreliable internet connectivity and power supply, can also hinder the growth of fintech companies. To address these challenges, fintech companies must invest in robust infrastructure and work closely with regulators to create a supportive environment for innovation. The future of fintech in Nigeria looks promising, with continued growth and innovation expected in the coming years. Emerging technologies, such as blockchain and artificial intelligence, have the potential to transform financial services further. For example, blockchain technology can enhance transparency and security in financial transactions, while AI can provide personalized financial services and improve risk management.

Collaboration between fintech companies, traditional financial institutions, and regulators will be crucial to the sector's growth. By working together, these stakeholders can create an enabling environment that supports innovation, ensures consumer protection, and promotes financial inclusion. In conclusion, the fintech revolution has transformed financial services in Nigeria, providing innovative solutions that promote financial inclusion and economic development. Companies like Paystack, Flutterwave, and Paga have led the way, leveraging technology to create convenient and accessible financial services. Despite challenges, the future of fintech in Nigeria is bright, with continued growth and innovation expected to drive further advancements in the sector.

The fintech revolution in Nigeria has also fostered a culture of entrepreneurship and innovation. The success of fintech companies has inspired a new generation of tech entrepreneurs to explore opportunities in the financial sector. This entrepreneurial spirit is driving the development of new fintech solutions that address specific needs and challenges in the Nigerian market. For example, companies like Carbon and FairMoney are offering digital lending services that provide quick and convenient access to credit. These platforms use data analytics and machine learning to assess creditworthiness and offer personalized loan products. By leveraging technology, these companies are making credit more accessible to individuals and small businesses, particularly those who are underserved by traditional banks.

The rise of digital savings and investment platforms is another significant trend in Nigeria's fintech landscape. Companies like Cowrywise and PiggyVest are providing innovative solutions that encourage saving and investment. These platforms offer users the ability to automate their savings, invest in various financial products, and track their financial goals. By promoting a culture of savings and investment, these fintech companies are helping Nigerians build financial resilience and achieve their financial goals. Additionally, fintech companies are leveraging technology to improve remittance services. Remittances from the Nigerian diaspora play a crucial role in the country's economy, providing a vital source of income for many families. Fintech platforms like PayTop and Sendwave offer fast, secure, and affordable remittance services, enabling Nigerians abroad to send money home with ease.

The integration of mobile technology with fintech solutions has also been a game-changer in Nigeria. Mobile money services, such as MTN Mobile Money and Airtel Money, have become popular among Nigerians who do not have access to traditional banking services. These services allow users to perform various financial transactions, including sending and receiving money, paying bills, and purchasing airtime, directly from their mobile phones. By providing a convenient and accessible way to conduct financial transactions, mobile money services are driving financial inclusion and empowering individuals and businesses. The impact of fintech on Nigeria's economy extends beyond financial services. By promoting digital payments and reducing reliance on cash, fintech companies are contributing to the formalization of the economy. Digital transactions are more transparent and easier to track, which helps reduce tax evasion and improve revenue collection for the government. This, in turn, supports public investments in infrastructure, education, healthcare, and other critical sectors.

The role of fintech in supporting small and medium-sized enterprises (SMEs) is also significant. SMEs are the backbone of Nigeria's economy, accounting for a large portion of employment and economic activity. However, many SMEs face challenges in accessing finance and managing their operations. Fintech companies are providing solutions that address these challenges, such as digital payment platforms, invoicing and accounting software, and lending services. By supporting SMEs, fintech companies are driving economic growth and job creation. The potential for fintech to drive social impact in Nigeria is immense. By providing financial services to underserved populations, fintech companies are helping to reduce poverty and improve livelihoods. Access to financial services enables individuals to save, invest, and plan for the future, which can lead to improved economic stability and well-being.

Fintech solutions are also being used to address specific social challenges. For example, some fintech platforms are focused on providing financial services to women, who often face greater barriers to accessing finance. By offering tailored products and services, these platforms are empowering women to achieve financial independence and contribute to economic development. The future of fintech in Nigeria will be shaped by several key trends and developments. The continued growth of mobile technology, increasing internet penetration, and advancements in data analytics and artificial intelligence will drive further innovation in the fintech sector. Additionally, the expansion of digital infrastructure and improvements in regulatory frameworks will support the growth of fintech companies and promote financial inclusion.

Collaboration between fintech companies, traditional financial institutions, and regulators will be essential to ensure the sustainable growth of the sector. By working together, these stakeholders can create an enabling environment that supports innovation, protects consumers, and promotes financial stability. The role of government policies and initiatives in supporting the fintech sector will also be crucial. Policies that promote digital literacy, financial inclusion, and innovation will help create a thriving fintech ecosystem. Initiatives such as the Central Bank of Nigeria's (CBN) regulatory sandbox, which allows fintech companies to test their solutions in a controlled environment, are positive steps toward fostering innovation and ensuring regulatory compliance.

In conclusion, the fintech revolution is transforming financial services in Nigeria, driving financial inclusion, and promoting economic development. Companies like Paystack, Flutterwave, and Paga are leading the way with innovative solutions that make financial services more accessible and convenient. The impact of fintech extends beyond financial services, contributing to the formalization of the economy, supporting SMEs, and driving social impact. As the fintech sector continues to grow and evolve, it will play an increasingly important role in shaping the future of Nigeria's economy and society. By embracing innovation, collaboration, and inclusive growth, Nigeria's fintech industry has the potential to become a global leader in financial technology.

CHAPTER 7

HEALTHTECH INNOVATIONS: TRANSFORMING HEALTHCARE

Healthtech innovations are transforming healthcare in Nigeria, addressing critical challenges and improving access to medical services. This chapter explores the rise of healthtech companies, their impact on the healthcare system, and the future of health technology in Nigeria. Healthtech, or health technology, refers to the use of technology to improve healthcare delivery, patient outcomes, and overall health system efficiency. In Nigeria, healthtech innovations have been driven by the need to address significant healthcare challenges, such as inadequate access to medical services, high disease burden, and limited healthcare infrastructure.

One of the pioneering healthtech companies in Nigeria is LifeBank, founded by Temie Giwa-Tubosun. LifeBank uses technology to deliver essential medical supplies, including blood, oxygen, and vaccines, to hospitals. The company's platform connects hospitals with suppliers and uses data analytics to optimize delivery routes, ensuring timely and efficient distribution. LifeBank's innovative approach has saved countless lives and earned international recognition. Another notable healthtech company is 54gene, founded by Abasi Ene-Obong. 54gene is a genomics research company that aims to advance medical research in Africa by collecting and analyzing genetic data from diverse populations. The company's work has the potential to improve healthcare outcomes by providing insights into the genetic basis of diseases and informing the development of targeted therapies. 54gene's efforts have attracted significant investment and positioned Nigeria as a leader in genomics research in Africa.

Helium Health, co-founded by Adegoke Olubusi, is another key player in Nigeria's healthtech sector. Helium Health provides electronic medical records (EMR) solutions to hospitals and clinics, streamlining patient data management and improving healthcare delivery. The company's platform also offers telemedicine services, enabling patients to consult with healthcare providers remotely. Helium Health's solutions have been adopted by numerous healthcare facilities across Nigeria, enhancing the efficiency and quality of care. The impact of healthtech innovations on Nigeria's healthcare system is significant. By leveraging technology, healthtech companies have improved access to medical services, enhanced the quality of care, and increased healthcare system efficiency. These innovations have also addressed critical challenges, such as the shortage of healthcare professionals and the high burden of infectious diseases.

Telemedicine is one of the most transformative healthtech innovations in Nigeria. Telemedicine platforms, such as Kangpe and DoctorCare247, enable patients to consult with healthcare providers remotely via video calls, chat, or phone. This technology has been particularly valuable in rural and underserved areas, where access to healthcare facilities and professionals is limited. Telemedicine has also played a crucial role during the COVID-19 pandemic, allowing patients to receive medical advice and treatment while minimizing the risk of infection. Mobile health (mHealth) solutions are another important aspect of healthtech in Nigeria. Mobile apps and SMS-based services provide health information, reminders for medication and appointments, and support for managing chronic conditions. For example, the mDoc platform offers personalized health coaching and support for patients with chronic diseases, helping them manage their conditions and improve their health outcomes. mHealth solutions have increased health literacy and empowered individuals to take control of their health.

Healthtech innovations have also improved the management of medical records and data. Electronic medical records (EMR) systems, such as those provided by Helium Health, have streamlined patient data management, reducing paperwork and administrative burdens for healthcare providers. EMR systems enable healthcare professionals to access patient information quickly and accurately, improving diagnosis, treatment, and continuity of care. Healthtech companies are also addressing the challenge of medical supply chain management. LifeBank's platform, for example, ensures the timely delivery of critical medical supplies, reducing shortages and improving patient outcomes. Other companies, like Zipline, use drone technology to deliver medical supplies to remote areas, overcoming logistical challenges and ensuring that essential medicines and vaccines reach those in need.

The use of data analytics and artificial intelligence (AI) in healthcare is another emerging trend in Nigeria's healthtech sector. Data analytics can provide valuable insights into disease patterns, treatment outcomes, and healthcare system performance, informing evidence-based decision-making. AI technologies, such as machine learning algorithms, can assist in diagnosing diseases, predicting patient outcomes, and personalizing treatment plans. These technologies have the potential to revolutionize healthcare delivery and improve patient outcomes. Despite the progress made, healthtech companies in Nigeria face several challenges. Limited digital infrastructure, such as unreliable internet connectivity and power supply, can hinder the adoption and effectiveness of healthtech solutions. Additionally, regulatory hurdles and funding constraints can limit the growth and scalability of healthtech innovations.

To overcome these challenges, healthtech companies must invest in robust infrastructure, collaborate with stakeholders, and seek partnerships with government agencies and international organizations. By working together, these stakeholders can create an enabling environment that supports innovation, ensures accessibility, and promotes the widespread adoption of healthtech solutions. The future of healthtech in Nigeria is promising, with continued growth and innovation expected in the coming years. Emerging technologies, such as AI, blockchain, and the Internet of Things (IoT), have the potential to transform healthcare further. AI can enhance diagnostic accuracy, personalize treatment plans, and improve healthcare system efficiency. Blockchain can ensure the security and integrity of medical records and supply chains. IoT devices can monitor patients' health in real-time, enabling early intervention and better disease management.

Collaboration between healthtech companies, healthcare providers, and government agencies will be crucial to the sector's growth. By working together, these stakeholders can create a supportive ecosystem that fosters innovation, addresses healthcare challenges, and improves health outcomes. In conclusion, healthtech innovations are transforming healthcare in Nigeria, providing innovative solutions that address critical challenges and improve access to medical services. Companies like LifeBank, 54gene, and Helium Health are leading the way, leveraging technology to enhance healthcare delivery and outcomes. Despite challenges, the future of healthtech in Nigeria is bright, with continued growth and innovation expected to drive further advancements in the sector. By embracing emerging technologies and fostering collaboration, Nigeria can build a robust and dynamic healthtech ecosystem that improves the health and well-being of all its citizens.

The role of government support in the growth of healthtech cannot be overstated. Various government initiatives have been instrumental in creating an enabling environment for healthtech innovation. For instance, the Nigerian Ministry of Health has launched programs to support digital health solutions, improve healthcare infrastructure, and promote public-private partnerships. These initiatives have helped to create a thriving healthtech ecosystem that addresses the country's healthcare challenges. Furthermore, international collaborations and partnerships have played a significant role in advancing healthtech in Nigeria. Global health organizations, such as the World Health Organization (WHO) and the Bill & Melinda Gates Foundation, have supported healthtech initiatives in Nigeria through funding, technical assistance, and capacity-building programs. These collaborations have facilitated the transfer of technology and knowledge, contributing to the growth and development of Nigeria's healthtech sector.

The impact of healthtech on patient outcomes and healthcare delivery is profound. By leveraging technology, healthtech companies have improved the efficiency and effectiveness of healthcare services, leading to better patient outcomes. For example, telemedicine platforms have reduced the need for patients to travel long distances to access medical care, improving access to healthcare and reducing the burden on healthcare facilities. Healthtech innovations have also played a crucial role in addressing public health challenges in Nigeria. During the COVID-19 pandemic, healthtech solutions were instrumental in supporting the public health response. Telemedicine platforms provided remote consultations, mHealth solutions delivered health information and updates, and data analytics tools helped track the spread of the virus and inform policy decisions. These innovations demonstrated the potential of healthtech to address public health emergencies and improve overall health system resilience.

The role of healthtech in promoting health equity is another critical aspect. Healthtech solutions have the potential to bridge the gap in access to healthcare services, particularly for underserved populations in rural and remote areas. By providing affordable and accessible healthcare services, healthtech companies are addressing health disparities and ensuring that all Nigerians have access to quality healthcare. The success stories of healthtech companies in Nigeria serve as powerful examples of the transformative potential of technology in healthcare. LifeBank's innovative approach to delivering medical supplies has saved countless lives, 54gene's genomics research is advancing medical knowledge, and Helium Health's EMR solutions are improving healthcare delivery. These companies have demonstrated that with the right support and resources, healthtech can drive significant improvements in healthcare outcomes.

In conclusion, healthtech innovations are transforming healthcare in Nigeria, addressing critical challenges and improving access to medical services. By leveraging technology, healthtech companies are enhancing healthcare delivery, improving patient outcomes, and promoting health equity. The future of healthtech in Nigeria is promising, with continued growth and innovation expected to drive further advancements in the sector. By embracing emerging technologies, fostering collaboration, and creating an enabling environment, Nigeria can build a robust and dynamic healthtech ecosystem that improves the health and well-being of all its citizens.

CHAPTER 8

EDTECH INNOVATIONS: REVOLUTIONIZING EDUCATION

Edtech, or educational technology, is transforming the education sector in Nigeria. By leveraging digital tools and platforms, edtech innovations are enhancing learning outcomes, improving access to education, and addressing critical challenges in the education system. This chapter explores the rise of edtech in Nigeria, highlighting key players, the impact on the education system, and the future of educational technology. Edtech refers to the use of technology to improve teaching and learning processes. In Nigeria, edtech innovations have been driven by the need to address significant educational challenges, such as inadequate access to quality education, limited educational resources, and a shortage of qualified teachers.

One of the leading edtech companies in Nigeria is uLesson, founded by Sim Shagaya. uLesson provides an online learning platform that offers video lessons, quizzes, and personalized learning plans for primary and secondary school students. The platform covers various subjects, including mathematics, science, and English, and is designed to make learning engaging and interactive. uLesson's innovative approach has made quality education accessible to students across Nigeria, particularly in underserved areas. Another notable edtech company is Tuteria, founded by Godwin Benson. Tuteria is an online tutoring platform that connects students with qualified tutors for one-on-one lessons. The platform covers a wide range of subjects and skill areas, including academic subjects, test preparation, and vocational skills. Tuteria's focus on personalized learning has helped students achieve their academic goals and improve their educational outcomes.

PrepClass, founded by Chukwuwezam Obanor and Olumide Ogunlana, is another key player in Nigeria's edtech sector. PrepClass provides an online platform that connects students with tutors for personalized lessons. The platform offers a wide range of subjects and test preparation services, helping students excel academically. PrepClass's success underscores the value of personalized learning in enhancing educational outcomes. Edtech innovations are not limited to K-12 education; they also extend to higher education and vocational training. Online learning platforms like Coursera, Udemy, and edX offer courses and certifications in various fields, enabling individuals to gain new skills and advance their careers. These platforms provide flexible and affordable learning opportunities, making education accessible to a broader audience.

Coursera, for example, partners with top universities and organizations to offer online courses, specializations, and degrees. The platform covers a wide range of subjects, including technology, business, and healthcare. Coursera's courses are designed to be accessible and affordable, making quality education available to a global audience. The platform's popularity in Nigeria reflects the growing demand for online learning and the potential of edtech to democratize education. Udemy is another online learning platform that offers courses on a variety of subjects, including software development, data science, and digital marketing. The platform allows instructors to create and share their courses, providing a diverse range of learning opportunities. Udemy's courses are often project-based, enabling learners to apply their knowledge in practical scenarios. The platform's user-friendly interface and affordable pricing have made it a popular choice for learners in Nigeria.

edX is a nonprofit online learning platform founded by Harvard University and the Massachusetts Institute of Technology (MIT). The platform offers high-quality courses from top universities and institutions worldwide. edX's commitment to providing accessible and affordable education aligns with the goals of edtech in Nigeria, making it a valuable resource for learners seeking to enhance their skills and knowledge. Edtech solutions are also addressing the challenge of educational content delivery in remote and underserved areas. Platforms like Eneza Education and OyaLabs provide SMS-based learning solutions that deliver educational content to students' mobile phones. These platforms make learning accessible to students who may not have access to the internet or digital devices, ensuring that no student is left behind.

Eneza Education, for example, offers interactive SMS lessons that cover various subjects and provide quizzes and assessments. The platform's focus on low-tech solutions makes it accessible to students in rural and underserved areas, where internet connectivity and digital devices may be limited. Eneza Education's innovative approach has improved educational outcomes for students who would otherwise have limited access to quality education. OyaLabs, founded by Boluwatife Ogungbayi, is another notable edtech company that provides SMS-based learning solutions. The platform offers personalized learning plans and interactive lessons that are delivered via SMS. OyaLabs' focus on accessibility and personalized learning has made it a valuable resource for students in underserved areas, improving their educational outcomes and fostering a love of learning.

The impact of edtech innovations on Nigeria's education system is significant. By leveraging technology, edtech companies have improved access to quality education, enhanced learning outcomes, and addressed critical challenges in the education sector. These innovations have also empowered students and teachers, providing them with the tools and resources needed to succeed. Edtech solutions have made learning more engaging and interactive. Video lessons, interactive quizzes, and gamified learning experiences have captured students' interest and motivation, making learning enjoyable and effective. Personalized learning plans tailored to students' needs and abilities have also improved educational outcomes, helping students achieve their academic goals.

Edtech innovations have also supported teachers by providing them with digital tools and resources. Online platforms offer teachers access to lesson plans, teaching materials, and professional development courses, enhancing their teaching effectiveness. Edtech solutions have also facilitated communication and collaboration between teachers, enabling them to share best practices and support each other. The role of government support in the growth of edtech cannot be overlooked. Various government initiatives have been instrumental in creating an enabling environment for edtech innovation. For instance, the Nigerian Ministry of Education has launched programs to support digital education, improve educational infrastructure, and promote public-private partnerships. These initiatives have helped to create a thriving edtech ecosystem that addresses the country's educational challenges.

International collaborations and partnerships have also played a significant role in advancing edtech in Nigeria. Global education organizations, such as UNESCO and the World Bank, have supported edtech initiatives in Nigeria through funding, technical assistance, and capacity-building programs. These collaborations have facilitated the transfer of technology and knowledge, contributing to the growth and development of Nigeria's edtech sector. Despite the progress made, edtech companies in Nigeria face several challenges. Limited digital infrastructure, such as unreliable internet connectivity and power supply, can hinder the adoption and effectiveness of edtech solutions. Additionally, regulatory hurdles and funding constraints can limit the growth and scalability of edtech innovations.

To overcome these challenges, edtech companies must invest in robust infrastructure, collaborate with stakeholders, and seek partnerships with government agencies and international organizations. By working together, these stakeholders can create an enabling environment that supports innovation, ensures accessibility, and promotes the widespread adoption of edtech solutions. The future of edtech in Nigeria is promising, with continued growth and innovation expected in the coming years. Emerging technologies, such as artificial intelligence (AI), virtual reality (VR), and augmented reality (AR), have the potential to transform education further. AI can provide personalized learning experiences, adaptive assessments, and intelligent tutoring systems. VR and AR can create immersive and interactive learning environments, enhancing students' understanding and engagement.

Collaboration between edtech companies, educational institutions, and government agencies will be crucial to the sector's growth. By working together, these stakeholders can create a supportive ecosystem that fosters innovation, addresses educational challenges, and improves learning outcomes. In conclusion, edtech innovations are revolutionizing education in Nigeria, providing innovative solutions that enhance learning outcomes and improve access to quality education.

Companies like uLesson, Tuteria, and PrepClass are leading the way, leveraging technology to transform teaching and learning processes. Despite challenges, the future of edtech in Nigeria is bright, with continued growth and innovation expected to drive further advancements in the sector. By embracing emerging technologies and fostering collaboration, Nigeria can build a robust and dynamic edtech ecosystem that empowers students and teachers and improves the quality of education for all.

The role of community engagement in the success of edtech innovations is another critical aspect to consider. Edtech companies that actively engage with communities and involve stakeholders in the design and implementation of their solutions are more likely to achieve sustainable impact. Community engagement ensures that edtech solutions are tailored to the specific needs and context of the learners they serve, increasing their relevance and effectiveness. For example, uLesson's approach to community engagement involves working closely with parents, teachers, and students to understand their needs and preferences. By involving stakeholders in the development process, uLesson has been able to create a platform that resonates with its users and addresses their unique challenges. This collaborative approach has contributed to the platform's success and positive impact on educational outcomes.

The potential for edtech to address educational inequalities and promote inclusive education is immense. By providing accessible and affordable learning opportunities, edtech solutions can bridge the gap in access to quality education for marginalized and underserved populations. This includes students in rural areas, students with disabilities, and students from low-income households. Edtech companies like Eneza Education and OyaLabs are leading the way in promoting inclusive education through their low-tech solutions. By leveraging SMS-based learning and other accessible technologies, these companies are ensuring that all students, regardless of their circumstances, have access to quality education. This focus on inclusivity is essential for creating an equitable education system that benefits all learners.

The impact of edtech on teacher professional development is another important consideration. Edtech solutions provide teachers with access to professional development resources, online training programs, and communities of practice. These opportunities enable teachers to enhance their skills, stay updated on best practices, and collaborate with their peers. By supporting teacher professional development, edtech companies are improving the quality of education and fostering a culture of continuous learning and improvement among educators. For example, platforms like Coursera and Udemy offer professional development courses for teachers, covering topics such as classroom management, instructional strategies, and educational technology. These courses provide teachers with the knowledge and skills needed to excel in their roles and support student learning effectively.

The role of data analytics in edtech is another emerging trend. Edtech platforms can leverage data analytics to gain insights into student performance, learning patterns, and engagement levels. This data-driven approach enables educators to make informed decisions, personalize learning experiences, and identify areas for improvement. By harnessing the power of data, edtech companies can enhance the effectiveness of their solutions and drive better educational outcomes. The importance of digital literacy in the success of edtech innovations cannot be overstated. Digital literacy refers to the ability to use digital technologies effectively and responsibly. As edtech solutions become more prevalent, ensuring that students, teachers, and parents have the digital literacy skills needed to navigate and utilize these technologies is crucial. Initiatives that promote digital literacy and provide training in digital skills are essential for maximizing the impact of edtech solutions.

In conclusion, edtech innovations are revolutionizing education in Nigeria, providing innovative solutions that enhance learning outcomes, improve access to quality education, and address critical challenges in the education sector. Companies like uLesson, Tuteria, and PrepClass are leading the way, leveraging technology to transform teaching and learning processes. The future of edtech in Nigeria is promising, with continued growth and innovation expected to drive further advancements in the sector. By embracing emerging technologies, fostering collaboration, promoting community engagement, and supporting digital literacy, Nigeria can build a robust and dynamic edtech ecosystem that empowers students and teachers and improves the quality of education for all.

CHAPTER 9

AGRITECH INNOVATIONS: REVOLUTIONIZING AGRICULTURE

Agritech, or agricultural technology, is transforming the agriculture sector in Nigeria. By leveraging digital tools and innovative solutions, agritech companies are improving productivity, enhancing sustainability, and addressing critical challenges in agriculture. This chapter explores the rise of agritech in Nigeria, highlighting key players, the impact on the agriculture sector, and the future of agricultural technology. Agritech refers to the use of technology to improve agricultural practices, increase efficiency, and enhance sustainability. In Nigeria, agritech innovations have been driven by the need to address significant agricultural challenges, such as low productivity, limited access to markets, and inadequate infrastructure.

One of the leading agritech companies in Nigeria is Farmcrowdy, founded by Onyeka Akumah. Farmcrowdy is a digital agriculture platform that connects farmers with investors who fund their farming operations. The platform provides farmers with access to funding, modern farming techniques, and market linkages. By leveraging technology, Farmcrowdy has improved agricultural productivity and created new opportunities for smallholder farmers. Another notable agritech company is ThriveAgric, co-founded by Uka Eje and Ayo Arikawe. ThriveAgric provides a platform that connects farmers with investors and provides them with access to funding, agricultural inputs, and market linkages. The company's focus on data-driven farming and precision agriculture has improved productivity and sustainability for smallholder farmers. ThriveAgric's innovative approach has earned recognition and support from various stakeholders in the agriculture sector.

Hello Tractor, founded by Jehiel Oliver, is another key player in Nigeria's agritech sector. Hello Tractor provides a digital platformthat connects farmers with tractor owners who offer tractor services on-demand. The platform uses GPS technology to track tractors and optimize their use, ensuring that farmers have access to mechanized farming services when needed. Hello Tractor's solutions have increased efficiency and productivity in agriculture, helping farmers achieve better yields. Agritech innovations are not limited to crop farming; they also extend to livestock farming and aquaculture. Companies like Livestock Wealth and Fresh Direct Nigeria provide innovative solutions that support livestock farmers and aquaculture practitioners. Livestock Wealth offers a platform that connects investors with livestock farmers, providing funding and market linkages. Fresh Direct Nigeria leverages technology to improve aquaculture practices, increase productivity, and enhance sustainability.

Livestock Wealth, founded by Ntuthuko Shezi, provides a platform that connects investors with livestock farmers. The platform allows investors to invest in livestock farming operations and earn returns based on the growth and sale of the livestock. Livestock Wealth's innovative approach has provided farmers with access to funding and market linkages, improving productivity and profitability. Fresh Direct Nigeria, founded by Angel Adelaja, leverages technology to improve aquaculture practices and enhance sustainability. The company uses hydroponics and aquaponics systems to produce fresh vegetables and fish in urban areas. Fresh Direct Nigeria's focus on sustainable farming practices has earned recognition and support from various stakeholders in the agriculture sector.

The impact of agritech innovations on Nigeria's agriculture sector is significant. By leveraging technology, agritech companies have improved productivity, enhanced sustainability, and created new opportunities for farmers. These innovations have also addressed critical challenges, such as limited access to markets, inadequate infrastructure, and low productivity. Agritech solutions have improved access to funding and agricultural inputs for smallholder farmers. Digital platforms like Farmcrowdy and ThriveAgric connect farmers with investors who provide funding for farming operations. These platforms also provide farmers with access to modern farming techniques, agricultural inputs, and market linkages, improving productivity and sustainability.

Precision agriculture is another important aspect of agritech in Nigeria. Precision agriculture involves using data and technology to optimize farming practices, such as planting, irrigation, and fertilization. Agritech companies like ThriveAgric use data analytics and remote sensing technologies to provide farmers with real-time information and recommendations, enabling them to make informed decisions and improve productivity. Agritech innovations have also improved market access for farmers. Digital platforms connect farmers with buyers, enabling them to sell their produce at fair prices. These platforms provide market information, such as price trends and demand forecasts, helping farmers plan their production and marketing strategies.

The use of data analytics and artificial intelligence (AI) in agriculture is another emerging trend in Nigeria's agritech sector. Data analytics can provide valuable insights into crop performance, weather patterns, and market trends, informing evidence-based decision-making. AI technologies, such as machine learning algorithms, can assist in predicting crop yields, identifying pests and diseases, and optimizing farming practices. These technologies have the potential to revolutionize agriculture and improve productivity and sustainability. Despite the progress made, agritech companies in Nigeria face several challenges. Limited digital infrastructure, such as unreliable internet connectivity and power supply, can hinder the adoption and effectiveness of agritech solutions. Additionally, regulatory hurdles and funding constraints can limit the growth and scalability of agritech innovations.

To overcome these challenges, agritech companies must invest in robust infrastructure, collaborate with stakeholders, and seek partnerships with government agencies and international organizations. By working together, these stakeholders can create an enabling environment that supports innovation, ensures accessibility, and promotes the widespread adoption of agritech solutions. The future of agritech in Nigeria is promising, with continued growth and innovation expected in the coming years. Emerging technologies, such as AI, blockchain, and the Internet of Things (IoT), have the potential to transform agriculture further. AI can enhance precision agriculture, optimize farming practices, and improve crop yields. Blockchain can ensure the transparency and traceability of agricultural supply chains. IoT devices can monitor soil conditions, weather patterns, and crop health in real-time, enabling early intervention and better management.

Collaboration between agritech companies, agricultural institutions, and government agencies will be crucial to the sector's growth. By working together, these stakeholders can create a supportive ecosystem that fosters innovation, addresses agricultural challenges, and improves productivity and sustainability. In conclusion, agritech innovations are revolutionizing agriculture in Nigeria, providing innovative solutions that improve productivity, enhance sustainability, and address critical challenges in the agriculture sector. Companies like Farmcrowdy, ThriveAgric, and Hello Tractor are leading the way, leveraging technology to transform farming practices and create new opportunities for farmers. Despite challenges, the future of agritech in Nigeria is bright, with continued growth and innovation expected to drive further advancements in the sector. By embracing emerging technologies and fostering collaboration, Nigeria can build a robust and dynamic agritech ecosystem that supports farmers and enhances agricultural productivity.

The role of government support in the growth of agritech cannot be overlooked. Various government initiatives have been instrumental in creating an enabling environment for agritech innovation. For instance, the Nigerian Ministry of Agriculture and Rural Development has launched programs to support digital agriculture, improve agricultural infrastructure, and promote public-private partnerships. These initiatives have helped to create a thriving agritech ecosystem that addresses the country's agricultural challenges. Furthermore, international collaborations and partnerships have played a significant role in advancing agritech in Nigeria. Global agriculture organizations, such as the Food and Agriculture Organization (FAO) and the International Fund for Agricultural Development (IFAD), have supported agritech initiatives in Nigeria through funding, technical assistance, and capacity-building programs. These collaborations have facilitated the transfer of technology and knowledge, contributing to the growth and development of Nigeria's agritech sector.

The impact of agritech on rural development is another critical aspect to consider. Agritech innovations have the potential to drive rural development by improving agricultural productivity, creating job opportunities, and enhancing the livelihoods of rural communities. By providing farmers with access to funding, modern farming techniques, and market linkages, agritech companies are empowering rural communities and contributing to economic development. Agritech solutions are also promoting sustainable farming practices. By leveraging technology, agritech companies are helping farmers adopt sustainable practices that minimize environmental impact and enhance resilience to climate change. Precision agriculture, for example, enables farmers to optimize the use of water, fertilizers, and pesticides, reducing waste and improving efficiency. Sustainable farming practices not only benefit the environment but also improve the long-term viability and profitability of farming operations.

The success stories of agritech companies in Nigeria serve as powerful examples of the transformative potential of technology in agriculture. Farmcrowdy's innovative approach to digital agriculture has connected farmers with investors and improved agricultural productivity. ThriveAgric's focus on data-driven farming has enhanced sustainability and created new opportunities for smallholder farmers. Hello Tractor's digital platform has increased efficiency and productivity in agriculture, helping farmers achieve better yields. In conclusion, agritech innovations are revolutionizing agriculture in Nigeria, providing innovative solutions that improve productivity, enhance sustainability, and address critical challenges in the agriculture sector. By leveraging technology, agritech companies are transforming farming practices, creating new opportunities for farmers, and promoting rural development. The future of agritech in Nigeria is promising, with continued growth and innovation expected to drive further advancements in the sector. By embracing emerging technologies, fostering collaboration, and creating an enabling environment, Nigeria can build a robust and dynamic agritech ecosystem that supports farmers and enhances agricultural productivity.

CHAPTER 10

CHALLENGES FACING THE NIGERIAN TECH INDUSTRY

While the Nigerian tech industry has seen remarkable growth, it faces several challenges that must be addressed to ensure sustained development and success. This chapter explores the key challenges facing the industry, including infrastructure issues, regulatory hurdles, talent gaps, and funding constraints. We also discuss potential solutions and strategies for overcoming these challenges. Infrastructure issues are one of the most significant challenges facing the Nigerian tech industry. Reliable internet connectivity, electricity, and transportation are essential for the growth and success of tech companies. However, many parts of Nigeria still struggle with inadequate infrastructure, which can hinder the adoption and effectiveness of tech solutions.

Internet connectivity is a critical issue, with many areas experiencing slow and unreliable internet access. This can limit the ability of tech companies to deliver their services effectively and restrict the adoption of digital solutions by consumers and businesses. To address this challenge, there is a need for continued investment in broadband infrastructure and efforts to expand internet access to underserved areas. Public-private partnerships can play a crucial role in improving digital infrastructure and ensuring that all Nigerians have access to reliable internet connectivity. Electricity supply is another significant challenge. Frequent power outages and unreliable electricity can disrupt business operations and increase operational costs for tech companies. Investing in alternative energy sources, such as solar power, and improving the reliability of the national grid are essential steps in addressing this issue.

Transportation infrastructure also affects the tech industry, particularly in logistics and e-commerce. Poor road networks and transportation systems can hinder the efficient delivery of goods and services. Investing in transportation infrastructure and developing efficient logistics networks will be crucial for the growth of the tech industry, especially for sectors like e-commerce and agritech. Regulatory hurdles pose another significant challenge for the Nigerian tech industry. Navigating complex regulations and obtaining necessary approvals can be time-consuming and costly for tech companies. Regulatory frameworks that are not well-adapted to the fast-paced nature of the tech industry can stifle innovation and limit the growth of tech startups.

To address regulatory challenges, there is a need for clear and streamlined regulations that support innovation while ensuring consumer protection and compliance. Engaging with stakeholders, including tech companies, regulators, and policymakers, to develop policies that foster a supportive environment for tech innovation is essential. Regulatory sandboxes, which allow tech companies to test their solutions in a controlled environment, can also be effective in promoting innovation while ensuring compliance. The talent gap is another critical challenge facing the Nigerian tech industry. The rapid pace of technological advancements requires a skilled workforce with expertise in areas such as software development, data science, and cybersecurity. However, there is a shortage of skilled professionals to meet the growing demands of the tech industry.

To address the talent gap, there is a need for continued investment in tech education and training. Enhancing the quality of tech education in universities, expanding access to coding bootcamps andonline learning platforms, and providing professional development opportunities for tech professionals are essential steps. Additionally, promoting STEM (science, technology, engineering, and mathematics) education at the primary and secondary school levels will help build a pipeline of future tech talent. Mentorship programs and industry partnerships can also play a crucial role in bridging the talent gap. Experienced professionals and industry leaders can provide guidance, support, and training to aspiring tech professionals. Collaborating with tech hubs, innovation centers, and educational institutions to offer practical experience and exposure to real-world challenges will help develop a skilled and ready workforce.

Funding constraints are another significant challenge for the Nigerian tech industry. Access to capital is essential for startups to scale their operations, develop new products, and expand their market reach. However, many tech startups face difficulties in securing funding, particularly in the early stages. To address funding constraints, there is a need for more investment opportunities, such as grants, loans, and venture capital. Public-private partnerships and collaborations with international investors can help mobilize resources and provide the necessary funding support for tech startups. Additionally, creating a supportive ecosystem that includes incubators, accelerators, and mentorship programs can help startups navigate the funding landscape and connect with potential investors.

The role of government support in addressing the challenges facing the Nigerian tech industry is crucial. Government policies and initiatives that promote digital infrastructure, support tech education, streamline regulations, and provide funding opportunities can create an enabling environment for tech innovation. Engaging with industry stakeholders and fostering public-private partnerships will be essential in driving the growth and development of the tech industry. Collaboration between the government, private sector, and international organizations will be crucial in overcoming these challenges. By working together, these stakeholders can create a supportive ecosystem that fosters innovation, addresses critical challenges, and promotes the growth and success of the Nigerian tech industry.

In conclusion, the Nigerian tech industry faces several challenges, including infrastructure issues, regulatory hurdles, talent gaps, and funding constraints. Addressing these challenges will require continued investment in digital infrastructure, tech education, and funding opportunities, as well as clear and supportive regulatory frameworks. Collaboration between stakeholders, including the government, private sector, and international organizations, will be essential in creating an enabling environment for tech innovation. By overcoming these challenges, Nigeria can build a robust and dynamic tech ecosystem that drives economic growth, creates job opportunities, and improves the quality of life for its citizens.

The impact of international collaborations and partnerships in addressing these challenges is significant. Global tech companies, international organizations, and foreign investors can provide valuable resources, expertise, and funding to support the growth of Nigeria's tech industry. For example, partnerships with tech giants like Google, Microsoft, and Facebook have provided Nigerian startups with access to global networks, mentorship, and funding. These collaborations have helped Nigerian tech companies scale their operations, develop innovative solutions, and expand their market reach.

The role of tech hubs and innovation centers in addressing the challenges facing the Nigerian tech industry cannot be overstated. These hubs provide a supportive environment for startups, offering resources, mentorship, and networking opportunities. By fostering collaboration and providing access to funding and expertise, tech hubs play a crucial role in nurturing innovation and supporting the growth of the tech ecosystem. In conclusion, the Nigerian tech industry faces several challenges, including infrastructure issues, regulatory hurdles, talent gaps, and funding constraints. Addressing these challenges will require continued investment in digital infrastructure, tech education, and funding opportunities, as well as clear and supportive regulatory frameworks. Collaboration between stakeholders, including the government, private sector, and international organizations, will be essential in creating an enabling environment for tech innovation. By overcoming these challenges, Nigeria can build a robust and dynamic tech ecosystem that drives economic growth, creates job opportunities, and improves the quality of life for its citizens.

CHAPTER 11

GOVERNMENT POLICIES AFFECTING THE TECH INDUSTRY

Government policies play a crucial role in shaping the development and growth of the tech industry in Nigeria. This chapter explores the various government policies and initiatives that have impacted the tech industry, highlighting their successes and areas for improvement. We also discuss the importance of a supportive regulatory environment and the role of public-private partnerships in driving innovation. The Nigerian government has implemented several policies and initiatives to support the growth of the tech industry. These policies aim to create an enabling environment for innovation, promote digital literacy, enhance digital infrastructure, and support tech startups and entrepreneurship.

One of the key government agencies responsible for the development of the tech industry is the National Information Technology Development Agency (NITDA). NITDA has been instrumental in implementing policies and programs that promote the adoption and use of information technology in Nigeria. The agency's initiatives include the National Broadband Plan, the Nigeria ICT Innovation and Entrepreneurship Vision (NIIEV), and the Digital Nigeria Project. The National Broadband Plan aims to increase broadband penetration and improve internet connectivity across Nigeria. The plan outlines strategies for expanding broadband infrastructure, promoting affordable internet access, and fostering digital inclusion. By improving internet connectivity, the National Broadband Plan aims to support the growth of the tech industry and ensure that all Nigerians have access to digital services.

The Nigeria ICT Innovation and Entrepreneurship Vision (NIIEV) is another important initiative by NITDA. NIIEV focuses on promoting innovation and entrepreneurship in the tech industry. The initiative provides support for tech startups through funding, mentorship, and capacity-building programs. NIIEV also aims to create a conducive environment for tech innovation by addressing regulatory challenges and fostering collaboration between stakeholders. The Digital Nigeria Project is a comprehensive initiative that aims to transform Nigeria into a leading digital economy. The project focuses on enhancing digital skills, promoting digital literacy, and supporting the development of digital infrastructure. By leveraging technology, the Digital Nigeria Project aims to drive economic growth, create job opportunities, and improve the quality of life for Nigerians.

The Nigerian Communications Commission (NCC) is another key government agency that plays a crucial role in regulating the telecommunications sector and ensuring the security of digital communications. The NCC's policies and initiatives aim to create a competitive and sustainable telecommunications industry, promote digital inclusion, and protect consumer rights. The Central Bank of Nigeria (CBN) has also implemented policies to support the growth of the fintech industry. The CBN's regulatory sandbox allows fintech companies to test their innovative solutions in a controlled environment, ensuring compliance with regulatory requirements while promoting innovation. The CBN's policies on mobile money, digital banking, and payment systems have also supported the growth of the fintech sector and promoted financial inclusion.

The role of public-private partnerships in driving innovation and supporting the growth of the tech industry is significant. Collaborations between the government and the private sector can mobilize resources, provide funding, and create a supportive ecosystem for tech startups. Public-private partnerships can also facilitate the transfer of technology and knowledge, promote digital skills development, and enhance digital infrastructure. For example, the Lagos State government has partnered with tech hubs and innovation centers to support the growth of the tech ecosystem in Lagos. Initiatives like the Lagos Innovates program provide co-working grants, accelerator grants, and workspace vouchers to support tech startups and innovation centers. These partnerships have helped create a thriving tech community in Lagos, often referred to as the "Silicon Valley of Africa."

The Nigerian government has also implemented policies to promote digital literacy and skills development. Initiatives like the Digital Literacy and Skills Development Program aim to enhance digital skills and promote digital inclusion. These programs provide training and resources to individuals and communities, ensuring that all Nigerians have the skills needed to participate in the digital economy. The importance of a supportive regulatory environment for the growth of the tech industry cannot be overstated. Clear and streamlined regulations that support innovation while ensuring consumer protection and compliance are essential for the growth of the tech industry. Engaging with stakeholders, including tech companies, regulators, and policymakers, to develop policies that foster a supportive environment for tech innovation is crucial.

Regulatory sandboxes, which allow tech companies to test their solutions in a controlled environment, can also be effective in promoting innovation while ensuring compliance. By providing a safe space for experimentation and innovation, regulatory sandboxes can help tech companies navigate regulatory challenges and bring their innovative solutions to market. Despite the progress made, there are areas for improvement in government policies affecting the tech industry. Ensuring the consistency and clarity of regulations, reducing bureaucratic hurdles, and providing adequate funding and support for tech startups are essential steps in creating a more conducive environment for tech innovation.

In conclusion, government policies play a crucial role in shaping the development and growth of the tech industry in Nigeria. Initiatives by agencies like NITDA, NCC, and CBN have supported the growth of the tech industry, promoted digital literacy, and enhanced digital infrastructure. Public-private partnerships have also played a significant role in driving innovation and supporting the growth of the tech ecosystem. However, there is a need for continued efforts to improve regulatory frameworks, enhance digital infrastructure, and provide adequate support for tech startups. By creating a supportive regulatory environment and fostering collaboration between stakeholders, the Nigerian government can drive the growth and success of the tech industry, promoting economic development and improving the quality of life for itscitizens.

The impact of international collaborations and partnerships in shaping government policies and supporting the growth of the tech industry is significant. Global tech companies, international organizations, and foreign governments have provided valuable resources, expertise, and funding to support Nigeria's digital transformation. For example, partnerships with organizations like the World Bank and the International Monetary Fund (IMF) have supported the development of digital infrastructure and promoted digital inclusion in Nigeria. These collaborations have facilitated the transfer of technology and knowledge, contributing to the growth and development of Nigeria's tech industry.

The role of tech hubs and innovation centers in influencing government policies and supporting the growth of the tech industry cannot be overstated. These hubs provide a platform for collaboration and engagement between tech startups, investors, and policymakers. By fostering dialogue and sharing insights, tech hubs can influence policy decisions and advocate for a more supportive regulatory environment. In conclusion, government policies play a crucial role in shaping the development and growth of the tech industry in Nigeria.

Initiatives by agencies like NITDA, NCC, and CBN have supported the growth of the tech industry, promoted digital literacy, and enhanced digital infrastructure. Public-private partnerships have also played a significant role in driving innovation and supporting the growth of the tech ecosystem. However, there is a need for continued efforts to improve regulatory frameworks, enhance digital infrastructure, and provide adequate support for tech startups. By creating a supportive regulatory environment and fostering collaboration between stakeholders, the Nigerian government can drive the growth and success of the tech industry, promoting economic development and improving the quality of life for its citizens.

In conclusion, government policies play a crucial role in shaping the development and growth of the tech industry in Nigeria. Initiatives by agencies like NITDA, NCC, and CBN have supported the growth of the tech industry, promoted digital literacy, and enhanced digital infrastructure. Public-private partnerships have also played a significant role in driving innovation and supporting the growth of the tech ecosystem. However, there is a need for continued efforts to improve regulatory frameworks, enhance digital infrastructure, and provide adequate support for tech startups. By creating a supportive regulatory environment and fostering collaboration between stakeholders, the Nigerian government can drive the growth and success of the tech industry, promoting economic development and improving the quality of life for its citizens. The future of Nigeria's tech industry is promising, with continued efforts to support innovation and create an enabling environment for tech growth expected to yield significant advancements and improvements.

CHAPTER 12

THE IMPACT OF THE TECH INDUSTRY ON NIGERIA'S ECONOMY

The technology industry in Nigeria has become a significant driver of economic growth, creating new opportunities and transforming traditional sectors. This chapter examines the economic impact of the tech industry, exploring how it has contributed to GDP growth, job creation, and the overall economic development of the country. The tech industry in Nigeria has seen rapid expansion, driven by increasing internet penetration, mobile phone usage, and a growing middle class. These factors have created a fertile ground for tech startups and innovations, which have, in turn, contributed significantly to the country's GDP. According to a report by the National Bureau of Statistics, the information and communication technology (ICT) sector contributed approximately 15% to Nigeria's GDP in 2020, reflecting the importance of technology in the national economy.

Job creation is one of the most visible impacts of the tech industry in Nigeria. The rise of tech startups has generated thousands of jobs, ranging from software development and data analysis to digital marketing and customer support. Companies like Andela, which trains and employs software developers, have played a crucial role in creating high-quality jobs and addressing the global tech talent shortage. Additionally, the growth of tech hubs and innovation centers has created numerous opportunities for employment and entrepreneurship. The ripple effects of job creation in the tech industry extend to other sectors, such as retail, logistics, and financial services. For example, the rise of e-commerce platforms like Jumia and Konga has created jobs in warehousing, delivery, and customer service. These platforms have also enabled small and medium-sized enterprises (SMEs) to reach a wider audience and grow their businesses, further contributing to economic development.

Tech innovations have also improved efficiency and productivity across various sectors, leading to increased economic output. In agriculture, agritech solutions like Farmcrowdy and ThriveAgric have helped farmers optimize their operations, increase yields, and access new markets. In healthcare, healthtech companies like LifeBank and 54gene have improved the delivery of medical services and advanced medical research, enhancing healthcare outcomes and reducing costs. The financial sector has also benefited significantly from tech innovations. Fintech companies like Paystack and Flutterwave have revolutionized payment systems, making financial transactions more accessible and efficient. These companies have also promoted financial inclusion by providing digital financial services to underserved populations, empowering individuals and businesses to participate in the formal economy.

The impact of the tech industry on Nigeria's economy extends to the informal sector as well. Mobile money platforms, such as Paga and Opay, have provided financial services to individuals who do not have access to traditional banking. This has facilitated transactions and savings for millions of people, enabling them to improve their livelihoods and contribute to economic growth. The tech industry's contribution to Nigeria's economy is not limited to financial metrics; it also encompasses social and developmental impacts. Tech innovations have improved access to education, healthcare, and other essential services, enhancing the quality of life for many Nigerians. Edtech platforms like uLesson and Tuteria have made education more accessible and engaging, while telemedicine platforms have expanded access to healthcare, particularly in rural areas.

Furthermore, the tech industry has fostered a culture of innovation and entrepreneurship in Nigeria. The success of tech startups and the support provided by tech hubs and innovation centers have inspired a new generation of entrepreneurs to pursue their ideas and create solutions to local problems. This entrepreneurial spirit is driving economic diversification and resilience, reducing the country's dependence on oil and other traditional sectors. Despite these positive impacts, the tech industry in Nigeria faces several challenges that need to be addressed to ensure sustained growth and development. These challenges include inadequate infrastructure, regulatory hurdles, and limited access to capital. The government and private sector must work together to create an enabling environment that supports innovation and addresses these challenges.

Investment in digital infrastructure is crucial to the continued growth of the tech industry. Improving internet connectivity, power supply, and access to digital devices will enable more Nigerians to participate in the digital economy. Additionally, addressing regulatory challenges and streamlining processes will encourage investment and innovation in the tech sector. Access to capital remains a significant barrier for many tech startups in Nigeria. Providing funding opportunities, such as grants, loans, and venture capital, will help startups scale their operations and bring their innovations to market. Public-private partnerships can play a vital role in mobilizing resources and creating a supportive ecosystem for tech entrepreneurs.

In conclusion, the tech industry has had a profound impact on Nigeria's economy, driving growth, job creation, and innovation across various sectors. By addressing the challenges and investing in the necessary infrastructure and resources, Nigeria can harness the full potential of its tech industry to achieve sustainable economic development and improve the quality of life for its citizens. The future of Nigeria's tech industry looks promising, with continued growth and innovation expected to contribute to the country's economic transformation. The expansion of tech-driven economic activities will play a pivotal role in enhancing the nation's competitiveness on the global stage, fostering inclusive growth, and unlocking new opportunities for generations to come.

CHAPTER 13

DIGITAL INCLUSION AND BRIDGING THE DIGITAL DIVIDE

Digital inclusion is a critical aspect of Nigeria's tech development, ensuring that all citizens have access to digital technologies and the opportunities they bring. This chapter explores the importance of digital inclusion, the challenges in bridging the digital divide, and the initiatives aimed at promoting digital literacy and access to technology in Nigeria. Digital inclusion refers to the efforts to ensure that all individuals and communities, particularly those that are underserved or marginalized, have access to and can effectively use information and communication technologies (ICTs). In

Nigeria, digital inclusion is vital for fostering economic growth, social development, and equal opportunities for all citizens.

Despite significant progress in expanding digital access, a substantial digital divide persists in Nigeria. The digital divide refers to the gap between those who have access to digital technologies and those who do not. This divide is influenced by factors such as income, education, geographic location, and gender. Rural areas, in particular, face significant challenges in accessing digital technologies due to inadequate infrastructure and limited connectivity. One of the primary challenges in bridging the digital divide is the lack of infrastructure. Many rural and remote areas in Nigeria do not have reliable internet access or electricity, making it difficult for residents to benefit from digital technologies. Additionally, the high cost of digital devices and internet services can be prohibitive for low-income households, further exacerbating the divide.

Digital literacy is another critical barrier to digital inclusion. Many Nigerians, particularly in rural areas, lack the necessary skills and knowledge to use digital technologies effectively. This lack of digital literacy limits their ability to access information, services, and opportunities available online. Gender disparities also contribute to the digital divide in Nigeria. Women and girls often face greater barriers to accessing digital technologies due to socio-cultural norms, lower levels of education, and limited economic opportunities. Addressing these gender disparities is essential for achieving comprehensive digital inclusion.

Several initiatives have been implemented to promote digital inclusion and bridge the digital divide in Nigeria. The government, private sector, and non-governmental organizations (NGOs) have launched various programs to enhance digital infrastructure, promote digital literacy, and provide affordable access to digital technologies. The Nigerian government has recognized the importance of digital inclusion and has implemented policies and programs to address the digital divide. The National Digital Economy Policy and Strategy (NDEPS) aims to enhance digital literacy, expand broadband access, and promote digital innovation across the country. The policy includes initiatives such as the Digital Nigeria Project, which focuses on training and empowering citizens with digital skills.

The Universal Service Provision Fund (USPF) is another government initiative aimed at promoting digital inclusion.

The USPF provides funding for projects that enhance ICT infrastructure in underserved areas, support digital literacy programs, and ensure affordable access to digital technologies. By targeting rural and remote areas, the USPF aims to bridge the digital divide and promote inclusive growth. The private sector has also played a significant role in promoting digital inclusion in Nigeria. Companies like Google, Facebook, and Microsoft have launched various initiatives to enhance digital literacy and provide affordable access to digital technologies. For example, Google's Digital Skills for Africa program offers free online and offline training to help individuals and businesses acquire digital skills. The program has trained millions of Nigerians, equipping them with the knowledge and skills needed to thrive in the digital economy.

Facebook's Express Wi-Fi initiative aims to provide affordable internet access in underserved areas by partnering with local internet service providers and entrepreneurs. The initiative helps bridge the connectivity gap and enables more Nigerians to access the internet and benefit from digital opportunities. Microsoft's Airband Initiative focuses on expanding broadband access in rural and underserved areas. By partnering with local providers, the initiative aims to deliver affordable and reliable internet connectivity, enabling more people to participate in the digital economy. Non-governmental organizations (NGOs) and civil society organizations have also contributed to digital inclusion efforts in Nigeria. Organizations like Paradigm Initiative and the Digital Grassroots have launched programs to promote digital literacy, provide access to digital tools, and advocate for digital rights.

Paradigm Initiative's Digital Inclusion program focuses on providing digital literacy training and access to ICT tools for underserved communities. The program targets youth, women, and people with disabilities, ensuring that marginalized groups can benefit from digital opportunities. The Digital Grassroots initiative empowers young people to become digital literacy ambassadors in their communities. Through training and mentorship, the program equips participants with the skills and knowledge to promote digital literacy and inclusion at the grassroots level. Despite these efforts, achieving comprehensive digital inclusion in Nigeria requires sustained investment and collaboration among stakeholders. Continued investment in digital infrastructure is crucial to ensuring that all Nigerians have access to reliable and affordable internet connectivity. Additionally, promoting digital literacy through education and training programs will equip individuals with the skills needed to navigate the digital world.

Addressing gender disparities and promoting the inclusion of marginalized groups is essential for achieving equitable digital access. By creating supportive environments and providing targeted interventions, Nigeria can ensure that all citizens, regardless of their background, can participate in the digital economy and benefit from digital opportunities. In conclusion, digital inclusion is a critical aspect of Nigeria's tech development, ensuring that all citizens have access to digital technologies and the opportunities they bring. By addressing the challenges of infrastructure, digital literacy, and gender disparities, and by implementing targeted initiatives, Nigeria can bridge the digital divide and promote inclusive growth. The collective efforts of the government, private sector, and NGOs will be crucial in achieving comprehensive digital inclusion and fostering a more equitable and prosperous digital economy. As Nigeria continues to advance its digital agenda, the focus on digital inclusion will be vital in creating a society where everyone can harness the benefits of technology, leading to a more inclusive and empowered nation.

CHAPTER 14

CYBERSECURITY AND DATA PRIVACY: CHALLENGES AND SOLUTIONS

As Nigeria's tech industry grows, so do the challenges related to cybersecurity and data privacy. This chapter explores the importance of cybersecurity, the risks and threats facing Nigeria, and the measures being taken to protect data and ensure digital security. Cybersecurity refers to the practices and technologies used to protect computer systems, networks, and data from unauthorized access, attacks, and damage. In an increasingly digital world, cybersecurity is essential for safeguarding sensitive information, ensuring the integrity of digital services, and maintaining trust in the digital economy.

Nigeria, like many other countries, faces significant cybersecurity challenges. The rapid adoption of digital technologies has exposed vulnerabilities and created opportunities for cybercriminals to exploit. Cyber threats in Nigeria include malware attacks, phishing, ransomware, and data breaches, which can have severe consequences for individuals, businesses, and the government. One of the primary cybersecurity threats in Nigeria is the prevalence of cybercrime. Cybercriminals use various tactics to exploit vulnerabilities and steal sensitive information. Phishing attacks, where attackers trick individuals into providing personal information through fraudulent emails or websites, are common. Malware attacks, which involve malicious software that damages or disrupts computer systems, also pose significant risks.

Ransomware attacks, where cybercriminals encrypt data and demand a ransom for its release, have become increasingly common. These attacks can cripple businesses and government agencies, leading to financial losses and operational disruptions. Data breaches, where unauthorized individuals gain access to sensitive information, are another major concern. These breaches can result in the exposure of personal data, financial information, and intellectual property, leading to privacy violations and financial losses. The increasing use of mobile devices and internet services in Nigeria has also expanded the attack surface for cybercriminals. Mobile malware and fraudulent apps pose risks to users, while unsecured networks and devices can be exploited for malicious purposes.

To address these cybersecurity challenges, Nigeria has implemented various measures and initiatives aimed at enhancing digital security and protecting data. The government, private sector, and civil society organizations are working together to develop and implement cybersecurity policies, improve awareness, and strengthen defenses. The Nigerian government has recognized the importance of cybersecurity and has established frameworks to address the growing threats. The National Cybersecurity Policy and Strategy (NCPS) outlines the country's approach to cybersecurity, focusing on protecting critical infrastructure, promoting cybersecurity awareness, and enhancing collaboration among stakeholders.

The Cybercrimes (Prohibition, Prevention, etc.) Act, enacted in 2015, provides a legal framework for addressing cybercrime in Nigeria. The Act criminalizes various cyber offenses, including hacking, identity theft, and cyberstalking, and outlines penalties for offenders. It also establishes the Cybercrime Advisory Council and the National Cyber Security Fund to support cybersecurity initiatives. The Office of the National Security Adviser (ONSA) is responsible for coordinating Nigeria's cybersecurity efforts. ONSA works with various government agencies, including the Nigerian Communications Commission (NCC) and the Economic and Financial Crimes Commission (EFCC), to implement cybersecurity policies and initiatives.

The Nigerian Communications Commission (NCC) plays a crucial role in regulating the telecommunications sector and ensuring the security of digital communications. The NCC has implemented several measures to enhance cybersecurity, including the establishment of the Computer Security Incident Response Team (CSIRT) to monitor and respond to cyber threats. The private sector is also actively involved in enhancing cybersecurity in Nigeria. Tech companies, financial institutions, and telecommunications providers invest in cybersecurity solutions to protect their systems and customers. These investments include deploying advanced security technologies, conducting regular security assessments, and implementing robust data protection measures.

Cybersecurity awareness and education are critical components of Nigeria's cybersecurity strategy. Various initiatives have been launched to raise awareness about cybersecurity threats and best practices. The National Information Technology Development Agency (NITDA) conducts cybersecurity awareness campaigns and provides training to individuals and organizations on how to protect themselves online. Public-private partnerships are essential for addressing cybersecurity challenges. Collaboration between the government, private sector, and international partners can enhance the country's cybersecurity capabilities and promote information sharing. The Global Forum on Cyber Expertise (GFCE) and the African Union's Cybersecurity Expert Group are examples of international initiatives that facilitate collaboration and capacity building in cybersecurity.

Despite these efforts, several challenges remain in addressing cybersecurity in Nigeria. These challenges include limited resources, insufficient cybersecurity skills, and the constantly evolving nature of cyber threats. Addressing these challenges requires continued investment in cybersecurity infrastructure, capacity building, and research and development. Investing in cybersecurity infrastructure is crucial to protecting digital systems and data. This includes deploying advanced security technologies, establishing secure communication networks, and implementing robust data protection measures. Enhancing cybersecurity skills through education and training programs will ensure that individuals and organizations are equipped to handle cyber threats.

Capacity building is essential for developing a skilled cybersecurity workforce. This includes providing training and certification programs for cybersecurity professionals, as well as incorporating cybersecurity education into academic curricula. By building a pipeline of skilled professionals, Nigeria can enhance its ability to prevent, detect, and respond to cyber threats. Research and development in cybersecurity will also play a critical role in addressing emerging threats and developing innovative solutions. Collaboration between academia, industry, and government can drive advancements in cybersecurity technologies and practices.

In conclusion, cybersecurity and data privacy are critical challenges facing Nigeria as it continues to embrace digital technologies. By implementing robust cybersecurity measures, enhancing awareness and education, and fostering collaboration among stakeholders, Nigeria can protect its digital infrastructure, safeguard sensitive information, and build trust in the digital economy. Continued investment in cybersecurity infrastructure, capacity building, and research and development will be essential in addressing evolving cyber threats and ensuring a secure digital future for Nigeria. As the digital landscape evolves, staying ahead of cyber threats will require a proactive and collaborative approach, ensuring that Nigeria's tech industry remains resilient and secure.

CHAPTER 15

THE FUTURE OF NIGERIA'S TECH INDUSTRY: OPPORTUNITIES AND CHALLENGES

As Nigeria's tech industry continues to grow and evolve, it faces a range of opportunities and challenges that will shape its future. This chapter explores the potential for further growth, the key trends driving the industry, and the obstacles that must be overcome to realize the full potential of Nigeria's tech sector. The future of Nigeria's tech industry is bright, with numerous opportunities for growth and innovation. The increasing adoption of digital technologies, the rise of tech startups, and the expanding digital economy are all positive indicators of the industry's potential. Several key trends are expected to drive the growth of Nigeria's tech industry in the coming years.

One of the most significant trends is the continued expansion of internet connectivity. As internet penetration increases, more Nigerians will have access to digital technologies and services. This will create new opportunities for tech companies to reach a broader audience and develop innovative solutions tailored to local needs. The growth of mobile technology is another important trend. Mobile phones have become the primary means of accessing the internet in Nigeria, and the increasing affordability of smartphones is expected to drive further adoption. Mobile technology will continue to play a crucial role in sectors such as fintech, healthtech, and edtech, enabling companies to deliver services to underserved populations.

Artificial intelligence (AI) and machine learning are poised to transform various industries in Nigeria. AI technologies can enhance efficiency, improve decision-making, and drive innovation across sectors such as finance, healthcare, agriculture, and education. For example, AI-powered solutions can provide personalized financial services, optimize agricultural practices, and improve diagnostic accuracy in healthcare. The adoption of blockchain technology is also expected to have a significant impact on Nigeria's tech industry. Blockchain can enhance transparency, security, and efficiency in areas such as finance, supply chain management, and digital identity verification. By leveraging blockchain, Nigerian tech companies can develop innovative solutions that address local challenges and create new business opportunities.

E-commerce is another area with substantial growth potential. The increasing popularity of online shopping and the expansion of digital payment solutions are driving the growth of e-commerce in Nigeria. As more consumers embrace online shopping, e-commerce platforms will continue to evolve and offer a wider range of products and services. Despite these opportunities, Nigeria's tech industry faces several challenges that must be addressed to ensure sustained growth and development. These challenges include inadequate infrastructure, regulatory hurdles, access to capital, and talent shortages.

Infrastructure remains a significant challenge for the tech industry in Nigeria. Reliable internet connectivity, electricity, and transportation are essential for the growth of tech companies. Continued investment in digital infrastructure is crucial to ensure that all Nigerians can participate in the digital economy and benefit from technological advancements. Regulatory challenges also pose obstacles to the growth of the tech industry. Navigating complex regulations and obtaining necessary approvals can be time-consuming and costly for tech companies. Streamlining regulatory processes and providing clear guidelines will create a more business-friendly environment that encourages innovation and investment.

Access to capital is another barrier for many tech startups in Nigeria. Securing funding is essential for startups to scale their operations and bring their innovations to market. Providing funding opportunities, such as grants, loans, and venture capital, will help startups overcome financial barriers and drive growth. Talent shortages are a critical issue facing Nigeria's tech industry. The rapid pace of technological advancements requires a skilled workforce with expertise in areas such as software development, data science, and cybersecurity. Addressing the talent gap through education, training, and retention strategies will ensure a steady supply of skilled professionals to meet the demands of the growing tech industry.

Collaboration between the government, private sector, and educational institutions is essential to address these challenges and create a supportive ecosystem for the tech industry. Public-private partnerships can mobilize resources, foster innovation, and drive economic growth. By working together, stakeholders can create an environment that supports the development of new technologies and the growth of tech companies. The future of Nigeria's tech industry also depends on its ability to adapt to global trends and leverage emerging technologies. By embracing innovation and investing in research and development, Nigeria can position itself as a leader in the global tech landscape. Initiatives such as innovation clusters, technology parks, and research centers can foster collaboration and drive advancements in technology.

In conclusion, the future of Nigeria's tech industry is filled with opportunities and challenges. By addressing the challenges of infrastructure, regulation, access to capital, and talent shortages, and by leveraging emerging technologies and fostering collaboration, Nigeria can realize the full potential of its tech industry. The continued growth and innovation in the tech sector will drive economic development, create jobs, and improve the quality of life for all Nigerians. The future is promising, and with the right strategies and investments, Nigeria's tech industry can achieve significant advancements and contribute to the global digital economy. By fostering a culture of innovation, promoting inclusive growth, and addressing the challenges that lie ahead, Nigeria's tech industry can become a powerhouse of technological innovation and economic development.

www.ingramcontent.com/pod-product-compliance
Lightning Source LLC
LaVergne TN
LVHW092233110526
838202LV00092B/19